Fueling the Fire:

The Battle for America's Energy Future

Steven R. Pottle

This book is dedicated to my wife, Nancy, and, daughter, Catarina. Thank you for all of your love and unwavering support.

Contents

List of Abbreviations & Acronyms

Full Text	Abbreviation / Acronym
American Wind Energy Association	AWEA
Barrel	BBL
Barrels of Oil Per Day	BOPD
Barrels of Oil Equivalent	BOE
Billion Cubic Feet	BCF
Billions of Cubic Feet Per Day	BCFD
British Thermal Units	BTU
Carbon Dioxide	CO_2
Department of Energy	DOE
Department of Defense	DOD
Energy Information Administration	EIA
Environmental Protection Agency	EPA
Feed in Tariff	FIT
Kilowatt Hour	KWh
Levelized Cost of Energy	LCOE
Liquefied Natural Gas	LNG
Master Limited Partnership	MLP
Megawatt	MW
Megawatt Hour	MWh
Natural Gas Liquids	NGL
Nitrous Oxides	NOx
Power Purchase Agreement	PPA
Parts Per Million	PPM
Renewable Portfolio Standard	RPS
Steam Assisted Gravity Drainage	SAGD
Sulfur Oxides	SOx
Thousands of Barrels of Oil Equivalent	MBOE

Full Text	Abbreviation / Acronym
Thousands of Cubic Feet	MCF
Trillion Cubic Feet	TCF
United States Geological Survey	USGS

An Important Technical Note:

Electric Power Generation versus Electric Power Generation Capacity

Throughout much of this book, reference is made to electric power plants or wind farms being of a certain size or capacity. A power plant, for example, might be referred to as a 50 Megawatt ("MW") gas-fired plant or a wind farm might have 50, 2 MW turbines for a total capacity of 100 MW. The key point here, however, is that these numbers refer to the amount of electricity that each plant can generate in only 1 hour. Therefore, in an extremely simplified case, where a 50 MW plant has absolutely no down time, its generation of electricity in one year would be 50 MW x 24 hours x 365 days or 438,000 MW hours. Readers who are residential consumers of power may be more familiar with kilowatt hours. In this example, a 50 MW plant running at full capacity would generate 438,000,000 kilowatt hours of power by running 24/7 for one full year (there are a thousand kilowatt hours in a megawatt hour). An important caveat is that power plants do not run at 100% of capacity all year round. This example is presented to illustrate the difference between generation capacity, expressed in MW, and electric power production, expressed in Megawatt hours (MWh) or kilowatt hours (KWh).

Preface

Over the course of most of my career, I have wanted to write a book about the energy industry. As I look back, the seeds of my energy business fascination were planted in the 1970's as I experienced, as a teenager, the United States' two major energy crises: the Arab Oil embargo and the revolution in Iran. April 18, 1977 brought a warning from then President Jimmy Carter; he lent insight to the energy crises and the need for American families to turn down their thermostats at home to conserve energy and to avert a larger energy crisis in the coming years and decades.

My career in energy finance has been a twenty-nine year journey that has taken me from my small hometown outside of Boston to multiple energy-focused jobs in New York City, positions in Dallas and Los Angeles, and a six-month assignment in Tokyo, Japan.

The following summary of my career is not meant to spend an inordinate amount of time dwelling on my career or achievements. After all, you are reading this book to learn about the battle for America's energy future, not to wade through a long recitation of my resume. However, I do want to establish that I bring to this book decades of experience analyzing energy companies, transactions, projects, markets and trends and hope that my background is reflected in the quality of the information and analysis in this book.

My professional career began at Swiss Bank Corporation, at that time, Switzerland's second largest bank. In 1985, Swiss Bank gave me the opportunity to specialize in energy finance, after having just graduated college. There I was, working in Manhattan and analyzing $25 million dollar or more loans originated by teams of senior bankers to energy companies across the United States. Twenty-five million dollars was unreal to me at that age. The hours were long, but I found myself elbow-to-elbow with great banking and energy finance professionals. I was also able to work in 4 World Trade Center: the low-rise building that stood in the shadow of the World Trade Center Towers. I then went on to hold energy finance positions with Swiss Bank (now UBS) in Dallas and Los Angeles through 1991. In 1992, I completed my Master of Business Administration degree from Southern Methodist University in Dallas, Texas.

Over the next twenty years, I also served as Vice President in various energy project finance and investment banking positions in New York with The Industrial Bank of Japan (Mizuho Financial), Deutsche Morgan Grenfell (Deutsche Bank Securities), Commerzbank, and HSH Nordbank. All were great experiences.

My twenty-nine year energy finance career has naturally led me to completion of hundreds of energy finance transactions; in total, these transactions total billions of dollars. These deals included credit facilities, term loans, synthetic (off balance sheet) leases, letters of credit and commodity and interest rate swaps (arrangements for hedging or reducing commodity price and interest rate risk, respectively). Also, while serving as an investment banker for a few years, I was a member of various teams pitching and completing a handful of bond issues, public equity offerings and mergers and acquisitions within the energy industry.

In the late 1990's, I also held the position of Vice President of Business Planning at Sithe Energies, a leading independent power producer. I have held energy finance positions in New York City, Dallas and Los Angeles, and, therefore, have covered energy companies and energy project developers from across the United States. In 2008, I founded Haywood Dorland Energy Capital LLC, a small private equity firm in New York City focusing on investing in conventional and renewable energy transactions and starting in early 2012 spent time with

Merrill Lynch as a Financial Advisor focusing on working with senior energy professionals.

In mid-2014, I founded Victoram Energy Research and Consulting, LLC. Victoram Energy offers a wide-range of consulting and research services. These include strategic planning, turnaround assistance, mergers and acquisition due diligence, assessment of new markets, energy trading credit risk management, fund raising, strategy assessment and development, etc. We are also developing a network of senior energy professionals who are available to fill key management roles (CFO, COO, and CEO) on an interim basis.

Energy companies that I have financed during my banking career included natural gas pipeline companies, oil and gas exploration and production companies, independent power producers, electric utilities and power transmission companies, among others. Projects and companies I have taken part in financing include:

- Refined products terminals or "tank farms"
- Electric utilities
- Oil exploration and production companies
- Natural gas pipelines
- Oil refiners
- A solar CPV company
- Offshore oil drilling platforms
- Electric power plants (projects)
- A biomethane plant in the Ukraine
- Numerous natural gas storage complexes
- Liquefied natural gas liquefaction facilities
- Ethanol plants

This book addresses various energy technologies. However, it is not a technical manual. It does not delve into the various engineering technologies related to hydraulic fracturing, wind power, or solar panel production. The technical areas of these topics are well beyond the scope of this book.

The analysis of the viability of the renewable energy sector in this book in the short and long-term applies only to the energy markets in the United States. Also, please be aware that the renewable energy sector analysis in this book is focused on utility-scale projects or applications. The analysis does not relate to small community-based wind and solar: homes and commercial applications that utilize less than 5 MW of generation capacity.

The shale revolution has already started to ripple through and cause significant changes in virtually every element of America's energy economy. As a result, a larger portion of this book is dedicated to explaining the changes. A smaller portion of this book is spent discussing the dynamics and outlook for the renewable energy sector. This is in no way meant to imply that renewable energy is less important than the shale energy revolution. It is, instead, just a reflection of the scope of change being wrought by the dramatic successes achieved by the shale energy sector. Also, the scope of the book's analysis of the renewable energy area has been limited to hydropower, wind and solar power. These energy technologies supply the vast majority of the renewable energy that is currently produced in the United States. Other renewable energy sources are either not as close as wind, hydropower and solar to being competitive with natural gas or are not scalable on a national basis as wind, hydroelectric and solar are. For example, utility-scale geothermal is very viable in areas like Nevada and California, which have geological structures favorable to geothermal development, but it is not viable across most states in the U.S. Tidal power, as another example, could one day be an important source of energy, but the technology is in its infancy and much more innovation is necessary.

Who should read this book?

I hope that this book will be of particular interest to energy company workers, managers and leaders in all sectors of America's energy economy. However, I believe that it is also useful to a wide-range of other professionals, such as:

- Executives in Energy Intensive Industries
- College Professors
- Commercial Real Estate Developers
- Financial Advisors
- Federal Agency Employees
- Members of Congress
- College Students
- Environmentalists
- Labor Union Members and Leaders
- Media Representatives
- Project Finance Professionals
- Venture Capitalists
- Individual Investors
- MBA Candidates
- Investment Bankers
- Commercial Bankers
- Pension Fund Managers
- Federal Energy Regulatory Commission Regulators
- Department of Energy Employees and Leaders
- Local Government Officials
- State Legislators
- Public Utility Commissioners
- Private Equity Fund Managers
- Auto Industry Executives

Researching and writing this book has been a very rewarding experience. I have outlined the shock waves of the shale energy revolution and assessed the outlook for renewable energy sources in a way that I hope is useful and insightful to energy industry professionals, leaders in other sectors of the economy and members of the general public who are interested in and concerned about America's economic, political and energy resource future. My writing goal remains to be positively objective about the relative strengths and weaknesses of the United States' energy resources—those both conventional and renewable. My great hope is that all readers will understand the next quarter-century of energy sector developments and the ways in which American lives and the energy economy will change: largely for the greater good.

Steven R. Pottle

Raleigh, North Carolina
October 2014

www.victoramenergy.com

Introduction

The United States is at a pivotal point in our nation's economic and political history. This opens up several questions about our future:

- Are we, as a country, facing an unavoidable decline in prosperity, competitiveness, and military strength?
- In the growing economic battle with China, do we find ourselves insufficiently armed?
- After the success of World War II and the Cold War, will we become the first generation to leave our descendants a weaker, less-affluent country?
- What role will energy play in restoring us to competitive strength and vitality?

After emerging from the Great Recession, we still maintain a relatively high unemployment rate. Also, almost 50 million Americans are on Food Stamps (now called the SNAP program). At the same time, the world remains a particularly dangerous place. Here in mid-2014, we see renewed battles across the Middle East, terrorists capturing more than half of Iraq, and a terrorist state, Iran, which continues to seek nuclear weapons. Meanwhile, Vladimir Putin seems quite determined to reconstitute the Soviet Union.

These facts are certainly alarming. However, what do they have to do with the American energy economy? Well, the United States' economic strength has always driven its global military and political strength. This need for economic strength is critically important in the future. What the United States urgently needs, therefore, is an economic paradigm shift. An economic game changer. Fortunately, it has arrived: it is the shale energy revolution.

At its core, the shale energy revolution is the innovation that has enabled the oil and gas industry to unlock huge quantities of new crude oil and natural gas resources embedded in large shale rock formations across the United States. This book takes you through the development of the shale energy revolution, including that controversial, but critically important and innovative technology – hydraulic fracturing. It also analyzes shale energy's impact on the coal sector, liquefied natural gas companies, electric utilities, and energy prices. The threat to OPEC is analyzed, as is the ability of the United States to become at least energy secure, if not energy independent.

Shale has been the oil and gas industry's version of the moon landing. Billions of new barrels of crude oil reserves have been found across the United States, our oil production has risen by millions of barrels per day, and we now have massive new natural gas supplies. No one could have predicted 10 years ago that domestic oil and gas production would be growing, much less booming. Now, Texas, North Dakota, and Pennsylvania are each world-class energy producers. The United States is a very real threat to the world's largest energy producers. Russia, Saudi Arabia and China, among others, are watching very carefully.

How far have we reached in the growth of the shale energy revolution? According to PIRA, an energy consulting firm, the United States became the world's largest producer of petroleum in 2013 (petroleum includes crude oil, condensates and natural gas liquids).[1] The country has also become a global leader in the production of natural gas, which is a central character in the story of the American shale energy boom. Natural gas is a clean, reliable, amply available energy source that will be the primary competitor to America's renewable energy industry for years to come.

Why does shale energy serve such a critical link to our economic future? Energy is the very bedrock on which the United States economy is built. Think of our great, sprawling country with more than 300 million people. We are a country of abundant natural resources, diverse industries, and nearly limitless innovations. And from our founding until today, we continue to have one fundamental need: energy. The energy needed to fuel the United States' $15.6 trillion economy. Energy to fuel our factories, our homes, our televisions, our cell phones, our vehicles, our very lifestyles, and, of course, the world's strongest military.

At the same time, however, America's renewable energy sector is far from standing still. Wind and solar power continue on their flight path toward "grid parity." This is a key inflection point where federal tax subsidies are no longer necessary for these energy sources to compete on price with electric power produced from natural gas and coal. Upon achieving grid parity, solar and wind power suppliers will be able to profitably sell renewable power at rates at or below current retail electric power prices.

This grid parity concept is likely to spark America's next energy revolution. It will change the competitive dynamics with all fossil fuels. Imagine explosive growth in solar installations across the United States. Millions of new homes and businesses opting to generate their own electric power and then selling their excess power back to their electric utility companies. Yes, it is already happening today across the United States, but far more growth is achievable.

So, grid parity is the Holy Grail, the Promised Land, the peak of Mount Everest for renewable energy. Will getting there be easy or inevitable? Can we just sit back and watch this optimistic scenario unfold, like an economic version of a reality television show? Absolutely not. Victory is certainly not guaranteed. Each of the main three renewable energy sources, wind, solar and hydroelectric power, will have their own difficult path as they fight to reach grid parity. Many challenges are ahead, including political opposition to tax incentives (subsidies?), high costs relative to natural gas, doubts about the threat of climate change and inconsistent access to the capital markets, to name just a few. Leaders across the renewable energy sector will need to laser-focus on innovation and reducing costs. The days of relying on tax incentives must come to an end.

A key wild card in the outlook for renewable energy in the United States is global warming or climate change. Can this book's author credibly opine on the validity of the climate change threat as if he holds of a Phd. degree in Climatology? No, he can't (and doesn't). However, it is clear that interest and concern about the climate change threat by the American public (and the politicians who represent us) has dissipated in recent years. Yes, core environmentalists are still heavily committed. However, millions of middle class Americans are now more focused on jobs, health care, taking care of elderly parents, paying for their children's college educations, and trying to save for retirement. Nevertheless, a dramatic change in the perceived urgency in dealing with climate change, perhaps due to more frequent natural disasters, would likely spur new initiatives to further promote renewable energy.

A handful of books have been written on the shale energy revolution. This book extends beyond that. It makes the case for seeing beyond today's shale energy headlines and imagining the potential for the United States' next energy revolution –renewable energy. The book also describes the status and potentially favorable outlook for three key renewable energy sources, wind, solar, and hydroelectric power. The book argues that America can, and likely will, become a world-leading producer of all types of energy within ten to twenty years.

Renewable energy versus shale: it is a relentless battle—one changing with every new innovation. Think of the classic corporate battles. You know them well. Pepsi versus Coke. Intel versus Advanced Micro Devices. Microsoft versus Apple. These seemingly intense competitive rivalries, however, pale in comparison to the growing battle between United States' oil and gas sector and our renewable energy sector. The outcome of this battle has greater stakes than these other, corporate competitions: this battle yields nothing less than the future of the United States' multi-trillion dollar energy industry, the country's standard of living, the careers of millions of our children, and (potentially) the health of the global environment.

The story of the shale revolution and the battle by renewable energy developers and companies to increase their competitiveness is ultimately a story about individual innovators and visionaries. These range from James Gordon of Cape Wind to Harold Hamm of Continental Resources to Charif Souki of Cheniere Energy to the late George Mitchell of Mitchell Energy, and include many others. Leaders and innovators at companies like Vestas, First Solar, Cheniere, Makani Power, Continental Resources, Tesla Motors and many others will mold and create the future of America's energy industry. These energy leaders and many others will benefit from innovation in a wide assortment of other industries, drive their own innovation and then benefit consumers of energy with cleaner, more cost effective and safer (militarily and environmentally) energy sources in the years to come.

Renewable energy proponents and shale revolution proponents are not, necessarily, friends. Renewable energy proponents often view oil and gas leaders as greedy, reckless polluters. However, oil and gas leaders sometimes view these renewable energy proponents as starry-eyed hippies—people with a misinformed view of the resources required to keep our nation revving with energy. If we are to transform America, we must set down our ideological clubs and work together to optimize all of the United States' vast energy resources.

A central question around all of the economic and energy policy issues is this: will America largely abandon dirty, carbon-dense coal and use clean natural gas as an intermediate-term transition to renewable energy or will we double down on fossil fuels and relegate wind and solar (and other renewable sources) to being niche energy sources? Could there be a plausible third alternative? Could the United States maximize both shale and renewable energy and become the world's energy giant? A key purpose of this book is to argue for the third alternative.

The United States and China are mid-battle for leadership of the global economy. Many analysts and pundits argue that the United States' reign as the world's economic superpower is nearly finished.

They say that China's economy will overtake the United States' over the next few years; the central world influence will shift.

This assessment is wrong. The United States can use energy as an economic weapon. We can lower costs across the economy in all of our key sectors. Already, billions of dollars of new investment in chemical plants have been announced. Natural gas exports via Liquefied Natural Gas (LNG) terminals will generate billions in export earnings (and crude exports should eventually be permitted). The United States, already the world's petroleum refiner, will have access to vast volumes of new shale oil. Tens of thousands of small businesses are already benefiting from the shale energy boom. Imagine if vast amounts of new, relatively inexpensive renewable energy is eventually added to the mix.

Are casual and professional energy industry observers stepping back and taking the long view of recent energy developments across the United States? Unfortunately, no. There is very often too much short-term thinking by analysts, politicians, consumers and even among some energy professionals with respect to changes in the energy sector. Many tend to mistakenly take the most recent 3 years of experience, whether low prices or declining demand or pipeline bottlenecks, and extrapolate this limited experience for years or decades into the future. For example, in the early 1980's many analysts and commentators said that oil prices would continue to rise indefinitely (they crashed in late 1985 thanks to Saudi Arabia flooding the market). By 2005, the threat of "peak oil" (and gas) caused many observers to believe that oil was going to $300 per BBL in the foreseeable future and that the United States would need to import increasing supplies of natural gas in the form of LNG. Oil prices, in part due to this growing belief in "peak oil", actually rose to $145 / BBL in July 2008. [2] The point is: the energy sector will continue to take dramatic, surprising turns, and we must not be myopic.

America must keep its strategic energy options open. "Expect the unexpected," although a cliché, is always a good guide when analyzing the U.S. energy sector. What events or circumstances could dramatically change our energy profile in a short five or ten year period? A major accident at a nuclear power plant, a determination that hydraulic fracturing causes major environmental damage (this is definitely not a prediction), or a crippling attack on America's electric power grid (causing homeowners to rush to distributed solar power, for example). Seem farfetched? Well, what was the perceived probability in the late 1980's that the Berlin Wall would be torn down and the Soviet Union dismantled? Who would have thought in the 1990's that Apple Computer would revolutionize the cell phone market and become a consumer products colossus?

Can you imagine an America just five or ten years from now that is a giant, world-dominating energy producer? A proverbial 800 pound gorilla in everything from oil to natural gas to solar to wind? This book describes the near term, dramatic developments that are occurring in the battle between renewable and shale energy resources and their implications for our life styles and economic prosperity. However, it also encourages you to step back from near-term developments and see the benefits and challenges we face over the next few decades. Through 2025 and beyond, a short time in the energy world, we are likely to make huge advances in our national interests due to energy innovation. These are likely to include gaining energy independence, boosting competition in our battle with China, reducing carbon emissions, creating millions of new jobs, generating huge export earnings, and further weakening OPEC's grip on America.

Part One:

The Shale Revolution

1

America's Energy Needs

Let's face it: Americans lead busy lives. And because of our driven schedules: our blaring alarm clocks followed by morning news programs, our steaming coffee before the drive to work, our endless workday followed by after-work child responsibilities, dinner responsibilities, and maybe a second to regroup prior to doing the whole thing over again; because of all this, we are lulled into assuming our energy resources are vast and undeniably available. We flip the lights on and flip the lights off without giving the truth behind our energy a second thought—without thinking of the almost 7,000 electric power plants scattered across the United States or the thousands of wind turbines. As you read this, there are tens of thousands of miles of natural gas pipelines, one hundred nuclear power plants, over two hundred thousand miles of electricity transmission lines, and one hundred and thirty nine petroleum refineries allowing you to casually go about your day.

The United States is in need of a strong energy economy--one that can lead us into a stronger global competitive position. Remarkably, the country's shale revolution has exploded in economic and competitive value in the past few years, despite developing during the 2008 market decline and economic recession. The collapse of Bear Stearns and Lehman Brothers, which were two large investment banks (combined with the very weak real estate market), nearly pushed the United States into an economic depression. Their collapse also caused a sharp cutback in renewable energy project financing. Also, despite the continuation of historically low interest rates continuing through mid-2014, unemployment across the country has remained relatively high. Further indication of America's United States need for a strong energy economy lies in the large number of American citizens collecting food stamps (now called the "SNAP" program). Approximately 46,097,090 people lived on food stamps in the United States as of March 2014.[3] Brought together, these people could fill a shocking 659 sports stadiums at 70,000 people per stadium. Even more drastically, this number equals almost four times the population of Portugal, an entire country (population: 10.5 million people). [4] Understand this: these numbers are not meant to make an ideological or political point. They highlight the importance of the shale energy boom at an economically challenging time in United States' history when countries like China represent a long term threat. Given the near paralysis of our elected political leaders in Washington it is reassuring, that a large segment of the private sector, namely the oil and gas industry, can lead the United States to greater economic growth.

Energy Demand and Efficiency:

Before the 1970's, the United States' energy demand growth was highly correlated with economic growth. However, United States' robust and diverse $15.6 trillion economy is increasingly energy efficient; essentially, we utilize less energy each year.[5] Since the 1970's, the United States has produced more economic output every year with less use of energy resources. The U.S. economy has grown substantially since the year 2000 and this economic growth has driven growth in demand for energy from 71.3 quadrillion BTU's in 2000 to 78.1 quadrillion BTU's in 2011; therefore, in these eleven years, our energy demands have increased just 9.6% with 51.4% growth in the economy.[6] (Note: a BTU is the amount of energy necessary to raise the temperature of one pound of water by one degree Fahrenheit. A barrel of crude oil has about 5.8 million BTU's).

Will the U.S. economy continue this favorable energy-efficiency trend? The U.S. Energy Information Administration projects that United States' average annual decline in energy intensity will continue through 2040.[7] This favorable trend continues despite growth in the number of cars and trucks on the road, an increase in the number of homes, and the millions of new personal computers, game consoles, tablet computers, and smart phones that American citizens enjoy.

From a practical, hands-on perspective, what drives America's huge need for energy resources? The following outline of our high standard of living illuminates the energy demand that over three hundred million Americans impose every day:

- 132,312,404 Homes[8]
- 3,900,000 Miles of public roads[9]
- 232,200,000 Cars and light trucks in the United States[10]
- 75,600,000 Personal computers for home use[11].
- 140,000 18-wheelers[12]
- 327,577,529 Cell phones[13]
- 1,513,548 Railroad freight cars[14]
- 5,724 Hospitals[15]
- 114,700,000 Televisions[16]
- 480,000 School Buses[17]
- 3,739 Commercial aircraft (over 90 seats)[18]
- 16,824,000 Recreational Boats[19]
- 9,477,243 Motorcycles[20]
- 1,300,000 Personal Watercraft[21]

Whereas the items above highlight the luxuries that we enjoy as a result of our advanced energy infrastructure and economy, there is a much more serious need for these resources: national security. The following section addresses the energy needs of the United States Department of Defense.

DOD: The United States' Biggest Energy Consumer:

The single largest energy consumer in the United States is the Department of Defense (DoD). Its giant energy consumption makes a lot of sense when you analyze the numbers. For example, the DoD supports the greatest number of United States' employees; it promotes 1.4 million citizens on active duty and an additional 718,000 civilian employees. Another 1.1 million people serve in the National Guard.[22]

The following figures highlight the enormous infrastructure owned and operated by the Department of Defense[23]:

- 2.3 billion square feet of building space
- 160,000 fleet vehicles
- 298,897 buildings within 500 installations across the globe

Fiscal Year 2011 brought the DoD global energy resource expenses to $19.4 billion. This equates to an average of $2.2 million dollars per hour.[24] It's interesting to note that the DoD's infrastructures are 99% dependent on the commercial utilities' electric grids (with a bit of back-up from electric generators able to provide a few days' power supply).[25]

The DoD presents leadership on energy issues by following a four-part strategy for reducing costs and enhancing energy security:

1) Decrease demand for fossil fuels
2) Expand supply of renewable and on-site generation (tied to microgrids and storage)
3) Enhance security
4) Leverage advanced technology

The federal government's budget allocates $1 billion toward energy efficiency in its 300,000 buildings.[26] This means, on average, only $3,333.33 is spent per building. Clearly, this amount is not enough to maximize the buildings' efficiency. Therefore, the government has adopted a sophisticated strategy of developing public and private partnerships; they enter into energy service contracts to improve the operations' energy efficiency without pushing federal government capital. The DOD's primary concern is energy resource security without immediate focus on cost. This concentration of efforts has enabled them to work with the private sector to advance the use of micro-grids, distributed generation, and bio fuels for fighter jets.

America clearly has an almost insatiable need for energy. Cheaper energy resources, whether from conventional resources or renewable energy, will allow America to drive further economic growth and innovation in the years to come. What this means is more jobs for our children and grand children, higher incomes for retirees (lower utility and transportation costs and maybe better stock market returns) and a stronger middle class (just ask the people in Pennsylvania, Texas and North Dakota).

2

Overview of the Shale Oil and Gas Revolution

Oil and gas industry geologists and engineers had understood the massive wealth hidden in shale rock formations for decades. Billions of barrels of crude oil and massive untapped natural gas reserves waited, untouched. The multi-billion-dollar challenge was discovering a way to drill for and produce these energy resources profitably.

The application of conventional, vertical well methodologies to shale deposits was historically too expensive in comparison to the profits derived from each shallow well. This is essentially because shale oil and gas resources are laid out beneath the ground much more horizontally than vertically. Therefore, utilizing vertical oil wells (that only drill one, vertical hole in the ground) in this age before horizontal drilling would have been a little like taking a straw and sucking the last one inch of a chocolate shake out of 30 nearly-empty glasses. It could be done, but one could not justify the effort.

The shale revolution—and more sound chocolate milkshake drinking—is possible with the combination of a relatively old, well-tested (pun intended) technology, hydraulic fracturing, and a new technology, lateral drilling. Lateral drilling allows for the initial vertical drilling; afterwards, the drills orientation can be turned ninety degrees for horizontal drilling. Hydraulic fracturing has been used since the late 1940's and lateral drilling has been developed over the last fifteen to twenty years. Although hydraulic fracturing is not new, the type of hydraulic fracturing operations and the utilized fracturing fluids adapted to the special needs associated with shale formations drilling are.

Shale Rock Characteristics:

So what makes extracting shale energy so difficult? In order to appreciate shale energy challenges and the requirements for hydraulic fracturing, one must have an understanding of shale's unique physical characteristics. Shale is simply a type of rock. According to the Encyclopedia Britanica, shale is "any of a group of fine-grained, laminated sedimentary rocks consisting of silt- and clay-sized particles."[27] Shale is the most abundant of the sedimentary rocks, accounting for roughly 70 percent of its similar rock type in the crust of the Earth.[28] Shale often lingers with layers of sandstone or limestone. These layers typically form in environments where mud, silt, and other sediments were deposited by gentle transporting [river] currents. Over time, these transporting currents compact layers together. Examples lie in deep-ocean floor, basins of shallow seas, river floodplains, and playas."[29]

If the following description of shale rock seems a little technical, please hang in there. It will enable you see just how difficult and challenging the shale revolution was to bring to fruition.

The crucial shale element impacting the shale energy revolution: after all of those transporting currents, combined with millions of years of pressure, the rock is very tight. Tight, in this context, describes the shale rock's very low permeability. Oil and natural gas do not move easily through this rock. "Tight", however, does nothing to describe the difficulty in removing the enormous energy resources from shale rock. In contrast to the shale rock, for example, sandstones associated with conventional oil and gas fields often have permeability in the range of .50 to 20.0 millidarcies (darcies and millidarcies are measures of permeability) while shale gas reserves, on the other hand, have permeabilities in the 0.000001 to 0.0001 millidarcies range.[30] Thus, shale is orders of magnitude tighter. To put this idea in context, think of beach sand or sidewalk concrete. Beach sand is roughly 2,000 millidarcies while construction-grade cement averages about 0.005 millidarcies,. Therefore, shale is far less permeable than beach sand or the concrete we walk over every day.[31]

Shale rock characteristics, which vary across the world, have significant ramifications for drilling, fracturing, and energy recovery. A specific formation of shale can determine, ultimately, how profitable each drilling and exploration operation is.[32] The extreme tightness and very low permeability of shale formations is the reason that drilling for and the recovery (called "development" in the industry) of these oil and gas resources is brutal. Hydraulic fracturing, however, has become critically important to the development of these colossal United States' domestic energy resources.

How extensive are America's new shale energy resources? Estimates of the United States' total technically recoverable shale oil and natural gas resources vary from organization to organization. This wide variability is due to a number of factors, including, but not limited to:

- The relatively short operating history of shale oil and gas production in the United States.
- The varying geographic location of the numerous shale basins.
- Rates of production declines varying across plays and basins.
- The amount of wet gas in each area included in the estimates.

The table below summarizes recent estimates of shale energy resources released by the United State's Energy Information Administration (6/10/2013): [33]

U.S. and Global Shale Resources: Table 2-1

(EIA Estimates)	Crude Oil (Billion Barrels)	Natural Gas (trillion cubic feet)
United States		
Shale oil and shale gas	58	664
Non Shale	164	1,767
Total	**222**	**2,431**

(EIA Estimates)	Crude Oil (Billion Barrels)	Natural Gas (trillion cubic feet)
Increase in resources due to inclusion of shale oil and gas	35%	38%
Shale as a percent of total	26%	27%
Outside of the United States		
Shale oil and shale gas	287	6,634
Non-shale	2,847	13,817
Total	**3,134**	**20,451**
Increase in resource due to inclusion of shale	10%	48%
Shale as % of total	9%	32%
Total World		
Shale oil and shale gas	345	7,299
Non-Shale	3,012	15,583
Total	**3,357**	**22,882**
Increase in resource due to inclusion of shale	11%	47%
Shale as a percent of total	10%	32%

Source: United States EIA. Analysis & Projections. June 13, 2013

Analysis of Technically Recoverable Reserves:

The Technically Recoverable Reserves of shale oil in the United States hones in at 58 billion barrels of crude oil. Each barrel is 42 gallons, and there are 58 billion of them. It's hard to imagine 58 billion barrels, sure. But we can agree that this is quite a bit of oil. In 2013, the United States consumed approximately 15.3 million BBLs of crude oil per day (not including natural gas liquids), or about 5.6 billion BBLs for the year.[34] How long, then, can the United States utilize the barrels of crude oil we can feasibly recover from our own land? If we assume a constant level of oil consumption relative to the 2013 statistics, the 58 billion barrels of shale oil reserves could meet United States' crude oil needs for approximately 10.4 years. Just ten years ago—a relative short time in the oil and gas industry—the idea that the United States would find 58 billion barrels of new oil resources was inconceivable.

The United States' conventional oil resources account for only about 5.5% of the world's oil reserves; however, its shale resources account for an impressive 16.8%. The United States is a world leader in shale oil development. We have developed the innovative technology and ramped up rapid production; but our relatively high percentage of in-house shale oil reserves doesn't hurt our percentages, either.

What about natural gas resources extracted from shale formations? Well, the estimate of United States' total shale natural gas resources of 666 trillion cubic feet is also incredible. If we assume constant consumption and an ability to recover and produce these natural gas resources, the math brings us to this: 666 trillion cubic feet of shale natural gas reserves divided by United States' 2012 consumption of 25.5 trillion cubic feet is equal to 26.1 years of supply.[35]

The estimated reserves divided by consumption ratio is a commonly used metric in the oil industry; it is referred to as the "reserves to production" ratio or the "reserve life" ratio. It's important to note that this estimated 26.1 year supply of shale natural gas does not include the estimated 1,776 trillion cubic feet of conventional natural gas reserves shown in the table above. Conventional gas reserves, therefore, would last an estimated 69 years (1,776 of conventional reserves divided by 25.5 trillion cubic feet consumed in 2012 is equal to 69.6 years).

Could the U.S. federal government estimates summarized above actually be too low? Well, the Potential Gas Committee, a group of 100 respected volunteer geoscientists and petroleum engineers, has released biennial assessments since 1964 revealing the total technically recoverable natural gas endowment of the United States. Their 2012 assessment shows estimated total shale gas resources of 1,073 trillion cubic feet.[36] Based on our country's 2012 natural gas consumption of 25.5 trillion cubic feet of gas, the estimated 1,073 trillion cubic feet of shale natural gas would last for 42 years. Keep in mind, of course, that the energy reserves that are technically recoverable are not always economically recoverable.

So, let's take a look at the bottom line for United States' energy investors, developers, transporters, and suppliers? We have an estimated 69 years from natural gas conventional reserves and a 42 year supply of shale natural gas. Therefore, our country has a potential 111 year supply of natural gas. Incredible.

Why, then, do we move forward with renewable energy? This data seems to be the death knell for renewable energy, right? Not in the least. The second half of the book outlines the many reasons why renewable energy will have a place in United States' energy future. We need to consider that the assumption that demand is constant—as demonstrated in the ratio above—is false. In fact, with new chemical plants, gas exports, continued substitution of gas for coal, and long term potential for growth in the use of natural gas to fuel all types of vehicles, our country's natural gas consumption could grow significantly—making that 111 year estimate a little meek.

Think of it this way: your fridge is stocked for the weekend. You have all the reserves you need to fuel yourself. But you don't expect to have friends over. When they suddenly appear at your doorway, your fridge suddenly depletes much more quickly. With more demand for energy resources, our country's stock of natural gas will decline. In this case, "calling for extra pizza" is a bit more complicated.

The Mighty United States' Shale Plays:

Seeing the immense catalogue of United States' shale energy resources is to understand importance of shale technology and its vast energy resources. However, it's best to dive deeper to the real story of United States' energy revolution. We must inspect the development of each of the major shale plays—places in which we can derive these energy resources.

The United States' well known shale basins are: Fort Worth, Texas' Barnett, Pennsylvania's Marcellus, Texas' Eagle Ford, North Dakota's

Bakken, and West Texas' Permian. Each one of these individual giant shale oil and gas plays would represent a massive energy resource for any other country. We, however, have the wealth of all of them. They are transforming the United States' energy industry; they are sending economic, political, and technical shock waves across the world.

Barnett Shale Play:

The Barnett shale play, located beneath the city of Fort Worth, Texas, is the mighty grandfather of all United States' shale plays. George Mitchell and his Mitchell Energy & Development Corporation (Mitchell Energy) engineers spent many years and millions of dollars innovating hydraulically fracturing in the Barnett shale formation. In the 1990's and early 2000's, when even modest-size conventional gas fields were increasingly difficult to find and expensive to develop, Mitchell and his team found and recovered an ocean of natural gas—right where everyone was already looking: natural gas' breeding ground in Texas. The discovery and economic development of the Barnett shale sparked an energy revolution.

Marcellus Play:

The Marcellus play was the second giant shale gas play developed by the oil and gas industry. It is centrally located in Pennsylvania, but it also straddles parts of West Virginia, New York, Maryland, and Ohio. The Marcellus is an enormous gas play. In Pennsylvania alone, there are currently about 4,000 wells producing natural gas.[37] Overall natural gas production reached 14.9 billion cubic feet per day (BCFD) in June 2014.[38] Therefore, Marcellus shale gas production boasts a daily production of about 2.5 million barrels of oil equivalent per day (natural gas converted to oil); this equation utilizes a gas to oil conversion ratio of 6 million BTU's per barrel of oil and about 1,000 BTU's per cubic foot of gas.

To understand the magnitude of the Marcellus play output, let's analyze a country: Nigeria. Nigeria is a member of OPEC, and it had average total oil production of 1.95 million BOPD in 2012.[39] Relate this to Marcellus' daily production of 2.5 million BOEPD. Therefore, the

Marcellus is producing more energy (on a barrel of oil equivalent basis) than the total oil exported by Nigeria, a key member of OPEC. Marcellus natural gas production could easily support an entire country.

Let's look at the money—always an important factor in relation to these shale plays. Natural gas prices are about $5.0 per MCF in mid-2014. However, the Marcellus shale production equates to $74.5 million dollars per day. That's $27.2 billion per year. Marcellus production is rapidly growing, as well. It is now more than 6 times greater than its production rate in 2009.[40] Just fifteen years ago, no one would have predicted that Pennsylvania would grow to become a leading producer of natural gas. Back in those days, Pennsylvania had the Philly cheese steak, the Steelers, and just lots of coal.

Permian Basin Play and Eagle Ford Play:

Texas, already an energy giant, is blessed with two enormous shale plays. West Texas' Permian Basin shale play (also called the "Cline" shale) is a giant shale oil resource. Unlike the oil production-focused Bakken or the natural-gas resource Marcellus, the Permian has significant production of both oil and gas. Oil production hit an incredible 1.5 million barrels per day in June 2014.[41] This rate of daily production is about 24% more than the 1.23 million barrels of oil produced per day by both OPEC members Ecuador and Qatar, combined.[42] Natural gas production in the Permian hit 5.3 BCFD in June 2014.[43]

The second giant shale play in Texas is the Eagle Ford. Although Eagle Ford is a relatively new play in terms of development, it is growing at an incredible rate. It stretches across 26 counties in South Texas, containing approximately 2,418 gas wells in 2013.[44] The Eagle Ford shale has a proportionally high amount of carbonate shale, honing in at about 70%. Higher levels of carbonate means that this shale is more brittle; therefore, it is easier to hydraulically fracture than other shales.[45]

The Bakken Play:

The Bakken formation in North Dakota's Williston Basin brings extraordinarily successful production of oil from shale rock formations.

Four northwest counties in North Dakota: Dunn, McKenzie, Montrail, and William contain 80% of the oil and gas wells.[46] Williston, North Dakota has become an absolute boomtown—not unlike the Houston building and population explosions in the late 1970's and early 1980's when oil prices more than tripled.

The Bakken formation has been a leader in shale oil production over the past 7 to 8 years. Bakken oil production hit 1,074,000 BOPD in June 2014 which is an increase of 14.9% from its 935,000 BOPD in September of 2013.[47] However, the Eagle Ford Shale in Texas recently surpassed the Bakken in oil production; it averaged 1,405,000 BOPD in June 2014.[48] This is surprising as drilling in Eagle Ford began only five years ago in 2009 versus Bakken's season premiere in 2003. Eagle Ford now rests at the second place ranking in countrywide production.

The great Bakken Play has elevated many sectors of North Dakota's economy. The trucking and railroad sectors have been booming. Trucks deliver the millions of gallons of water that are used in the drilling and hydraulic fracturing operations. Also, thousands of trucks and railroad cars are required to transport barrels upon barrels of crude oil from the Bakken to other parts of the United States.

Let's put some perspective on North Dakota's massive oil boom. Let's analyze the planet from outer space. From outer space, as you probably know, all the United States' major cities are in full view. New York, Chicago, Boston, Dallas, Houston, and Los Angeles are lit up like oncoming traffic on a desolate road at night. The satellite photo shows nothing of United States' rural and desert areas. However, the past few years have brought an incredible difference. If you focus your eyes on North Dakota, you will find a speck illuminated like a 5-million person city. This light is from the flaring of excess natural gas; it is reminiscent of a celebration on the fourth of July. Environmental note: it is actually much safer for the environment to flare unused natural gas than to release the methane directly into the environment. Methane is a powerful greenhouse gas.

There lies an interesting paradox in North Dakota's wildly successful oil and gas development, however. The state is also a leader in wind power production. There are huge wind farms scattered all across the state.

No one could have imagined fifteen years ago that North Dakota would become a national leader in both wind power and crude oil production. Some Americans might have a hard time pointing North Dakota out on a map! However, the state's wind resource ranks third among all states in the percentage of wind-supplied power (about 15%).[49] Energy developers are focused on developing wind energy projects in North Dakota, the center of one of United States' key shale oil booms. Could North Dakota be a model for other states in terms of developing significant energy resources in both the renewable and conventional energy arenas?

Monterey Play:

The last major shale play in the United States is California's Monterey. Because of Californian hydraulic fracturing restrictions, this play has had very little development. Table 2-2 shown below lists potential Total Technically Recoverable reserves of 15 billion barrels in the state of California; 13.7 billion barrels of these 15 billion were estimated to be in the Monterey formation. In May 2014, however, America's Energy Information Administration announced a revision to its estimates of the Monterey's Technically Recoverable Reserves to only 600 million barrels.[50] This is quite a drastic reduction.

This drastic estimate reduction is based on EIA's original assumption that the Monterey shale's characteristics were similar to those in the Bakken and Eagle Ford shale areas.[51] However, once the drilling began and production rates were measured, the Monterey formation geology turned out to be very different and more challenging.[52]

Clearly, this was not good news for the oil and gas industry. Some anti-shale, anti-fracking analysts and pundits quickly jumped on this news to claim that the narrative of California oil's being a major contributor on the United States' path to energy security was no longer valid. However, the geology hindrance is just one more technical challenge that must be overcome by the oil and gas industry. The oil is still there. The industry must develop new technology to optimize production for this specific type of shale formation. It will take time, capital, and innovation. However, the oil and gas industry has a strong record of meeting just these types of technical challenges.

The following table provides a ranking of the biggest and most important shale plays in the United States:

Key United States Shale Plays: Table 2-2

	Location	Shale Gas Resources (TCF)*	Percent of Gas Total	Shale Oil Resources (Billion BBLS)*	Percent of Oil Total
Marcellus	Pennsylvania, West Virginia, Ohio, New York	410.0	54.0	0.0	0.0
Haynesville	Arkansas, Louisiana, Texas	75.0	10.0	0.0	0.0
Barnett	Texas	43.0	5.7	0.0	0.0
Barnett Woodford	Texas	32.0	4.3	0.0	0.0
Monterey / Santos	California	0.0	0.0	15.0	62.5
Bakken	North Dakota, Montana, Canada	0.0	0.0	4.0	16.7
Eagle Ford	Texas	21.0	0.0	3.0	12.5
Other Plays	Miscellaneous	169.0	26%	2.0	8.3
Total		750.0	100%	24.0	100%

Source: U.S. Energy Information Administration. * Technically recoverable reserves. Review of Emerging Resources: U.S. Shale Gas and Shale Oil Plays, July, 2011. The estimates of total technically recoverable reserves in the above table vary from the global estimates presented elsewhere in this chapter. The global data in Table 2-1 is more recent than the above estimates broken out by each specific shale play.

The table above estimates Technically Recoverable Reserves for shale plays, or the total amount of oil and gas resources that can potentially be produced using today's technology. These numbers are irrespective of market price or drilling costs; they hold no regard to profitability. If natural gas prices fell to $1.0 per MCF, for example, very little of this gas would be profitable, but the reserves would still be technically recoverable.

Proved Reserves:

Proved reserves, which is a higher standard in categorizing oil and gas reserves, are the estimated amounts of oil and gas that can be produced using today's technology and today's market price. In other words, the sale of the oil and gas needs to be at or above the breakeven price or profitable. Reserves get "proved up" over time through the drilling of additional wells, the measurement of production, and their associated decline rates. Oil and gas wells start out with high initial production rates (barrels per day, for example) and decline over time due to loss of pressure built up in the oil and gas reservoirs.

Within mature, conventional natural gas fields, it is not uncommon to see small annual increases in production with level or even declining reserves. However, the shale basins are just the opposite. The shale basins are very new properties that are "proved up" rapidly through extensive drilling across each major play. As each well is completed and production rates are tested, a clearer picture emerges of the ultimate size of each field or play's proven reserves. Given the already incredible estimates of total technically recoverable reserves for many of these plays, it is likely that total production and proven reserves will grow rapidly in the coming years—assuming, of course, that oil and natural gas prices remain relatively stable.

Estimated proved natural gas reserves as of the end of 2012 (measured in trillions of cubic feet) are found in the table below. The numbers will tend to be low as a result of the novel drilling operations.

Shale Gas Reserves and Production: Table 2-3

Shale Gas Play (TCF)	2011 Production	2012 Production	Percent Change in Production	2011 Proved Reserves	2012 Proved Reserves	Percent Change in Reserves
Marcellus	1.4	2.4	71.4	31.9	42.8	34.2

Shale Gas Play (TCF)	2011 Pro-duction	2012 Pro-duction	Percent Change in Pro-duction	2011 Proved Reserves	2012 Proved Reserves	Percent Change in Reserves
Barnett	2.0	2.0	0.0	32.6	23.7	-27.3
Haynesville / Bossier	2.5	2.7	8.0	29.5	17.7	-40.0
Eagle Ford	0.4	0.9	125.0	8.4	16.2	92.9
Woodford	0.5	0.6	20.0	10.8	11.1	2.8
Fayetteville	0.9	1.0	11.1	14.8	9.7	-34.5
Other	0.3	0.8	166.6	3.6	8.2	127.7
Total	**8.0**	**10.4**	**30.0%**	**131.6**	**129.4**	**-1.7%**

Source: Energy Information Administration, "U.S. Crude Oil and Natural Gas Proven Reserves"

Some of the data above may seem counterintuitive and inconsistent with the theme of the shale energy revolution. Specifically, while production rose dramatically in almost all of the shale plays, the proven reserves fell sharply in some of the key shale areas. How does this happen?

Essentially, proven reserves are a function of a number of different variables. Two of the most important variables involve the quantity of reserves and the market price of natural gas and/or oil. In some of the more gas oriented plays above, like the Barnett, proven reserves fell sharply in 2012. This is because Barnett is a mature area compared to the other plays; therefore, the general quantity of the reserves is already identified and understood. There are sharp increases in the other plays because exploration revealed greater understanding of the play's resource quantities. Also, a significant downward pressure on proved reserves was the sharp drop in natural gas prices during the year. The Marcellus and the Eagle Ford, for example, had such strong growth in the quantity of discovered natural gas that it more than compensated for the negative impact of lower natural gas prices. Low gas prices, of course, were the result of the widespread success in finding new shale gas reserves in the first place.

Shale Oil Reserves and Production: Table 2-4

Shale Oil Plays (Millions of Barrels)	2011 Pro- duction	2012 Pro- duction	Percent Change in Pro- duction	2011 Proved Reserves	2012 Proved Reserves	Percent Change in Re- serves
Eagle Ford	71.0	209.0	194.4	1,251.0	3,372.0	169.5
Bakken	123.0	213.0	73.2	1,998.0	3,166.0	58.5
Barnett	8.0	10.0	25.0	118.0	66.0	-44.1
Marcellus	0.0	4.0	NA	0.0	72.0	NA
Niobrara	2.0	3.0	50.0	8.0	14.0	75.0
Other	24.0	41.0	70.8	253.0	648.0	156.1
Total	**228.0**	**480.0**	**110.5**	**3,628.0**	**7,338.0**	**102.3**

Source: Energy Information Administration Source: Energy Information Administration, "U.S. Crude Oil and Natural Gas Proven Reserves"

Because oil prices are determined globally, the United States' 2011 and 2012 rapid increase in oil production did not depress oil prices. Compare this to the national determination of the United States' natural gas prices. When there is a great increase in natural gas production, domestic gas prices decline.

The reserves and production percentage changes in the table above are somewhat misleading. One could see them and simply say that both reserves and production went up by about 100%. The absolute numbers, however, tell the real story. Oil and gas production reduces the amount of available resources while exploration adds to the resource base. For much of the later part of the 20th century, oil and gas companies struggled to replace 100% of production each year with new proved reserves. Exploration was not fruitful. In 2012, everything was incredibly different. 480 million barrels of shale oil were produced in the United States in that year, while an additional 3,710 million barrels of shale oil was found via exploration. These 3,710 million barrels were added to our country's oil proved resource base. Essentially, hopes for major new oil reserves were restored.

A Bit of History and a Worldwide Comparison:

The shale revolution began quite a long time ago. In 1821, a full 38 years before Colonel Edwin Drake drilled his famous oil well in Titusville, Pennsylvania, a Fredonia, New York gunsmith named William Hart became the first person to drill a natural gas well in shale rock.[53] Hart placed a primitive gas meter on the 70 foot deep well and delivered the natural gas via pipeline to a nearby inn located on the Buffalo, New York to Cleveland, Ohio stagecoach line.[54]

Estimated United States shale oil and gas resources with the addition of 41 other countries' 137 shale formations represent 10% of the world's total crude oil and 32% of the world's technically recoverable reserve natural gas.[55] More than half of the identified shale oil resources outside of the United States are concentrated in five countries: China, Argentina, Algeria, Canada, and Mexico.[56] When comparing the United States to the 41 other shale oil resource countries around the world, we rank second only after Russia in shale oil resources and fourth after Algeria for shale gas resources.[57]

The table below summarizes the top ten estimated Technically Recoverable shale reserves in various countries around the world:

Global Technically Recoverable Shale Reserves: Table 2-5

Shale Oil			Shale Gas		
Rank	Country	Shale Oil (Billion BBLs)	Rank	Country	Shale Gas (TCF)
1	Russia	75	1	China	1,115
2	U.S.	58	2	Argentina	802
3	China	32	3	Algeria	707
4	Argentina	27	4	U.S.	665
5	Libya	26	5	Canada	573
6	Australia	18	6	Mexico	545

Shale Oil			Shale Gas		
7	Venezuela	13	7	Australia	437
8	Mexico	13	8	South Africa	390
Rank	**Country**	**Shale Oil (Billion BBLs)**	**Rank**	**Country**	**Shale Gas (TCF)**
9	Pakistan	9	9	Russia	285
10	Canada	9	10	Brazil	245
World Total		**280**			**5764**

Source: U.S. Energy Information Administration, "Today in Energy", June 10, 2013.

Innovation in the American shale energy sector is rippling across the globe, impacting countries around the world. From Poland to China to South Africa, countries are finding significant new energy reserves that will significantly impact regional economies and change the balance of military power. The United States is leading the advanced technologically.

Natural gas dominates the shale revolution news. This is because the United States is already nearly self-sufficient in our natural gas supply. Therefore, more sources of clean energy can create displacement of dirty fuels like coal. What makes shale natural gas a clean and valuable energy source? In general, there are four key characteristics that make a particular source of energy valuable. Incredibly, shale natural gas has all four of these:

Key Natural Gas Characteristics: Table 2-6

Characteristic	Details
Affordable	Shale gas supplies have put significant downward pressure on natural gas prices, with costs now averaging around $5/mm BTU's.
Available	With numerous large shale basins across the U.S., like the Barnett and the Marcellus, shale gas supplies are very prolific.

Characteristic	Details
Reliable	Shale gas supplies are domestic, geographically scattered across the United States, and have access to hundreds of thousands of miles of existing pipeline infrastructure. They are, therefore, very reliable.
Clean	The burning of natural gas results in only about ½ of the carbon dioxide emissions associated with the burning of coal, its main competitor for the production of electricity. The replacement of coal with shale natural gas is a clear victory for the environment (putting aside for a moment the environmental allegations surrounding hydraulic fracturing).

Incredible American Need for Natural Gas:

It is hard to overestimate the importance of natural gas in meeting Americans' energy needs. Approximately 65,000,000 homes in the United States use natural gas for space and water heating while approximately 98% of homes have access to electric power. An increasing portion of electric power is natural gas generated.[58]

An instructive example of the tangible benefits derived from the increased use of natural gas is found in New York City, home to approximately eight million Americans. New York City's air quality is better than it has been in the last fifty years.[59] According to a press release issued by former Mayor Bloomberg's office on September 26, 2013: "Three changes contributed to the winter season air quality improvements over the past several years. Only three years ago, nearly 10,000 buildings in New York City burned Numbers 4 and 6 heating oil, which emit significant amounts of soot pollution (PM2.5), sulfur dioxide (SO_2), nickel, and other dangerous pollutants. Through the efforts of the NYC Clean Heat Program, over 2,700 buildings have converted to cleaner fuels (natural gas) since 2011 and an additional 2,500 buildings are actively pursuing conversions. Second, additional emission reductions have come from State rules that limited the sulfur content of #2 heating oil to 15 parts per million (a 99 percent reduction) and City rules restricting the sulfur content of #4 oil to 1,500 parts per million (a 50% reduction). Third, the expansion of the regional natural gas supply and local gas distribution infrastructure operated by Con Edison and National Grid has encouraged buildings to save money and reduce emissions by converting to natural gas. As a result, citywide concentrations of SO_2 have declined by 69 percent and nickel by 35 percent. Neighborhoods with the highest density of emissions reductions from boiler conversions – such as northern Manhattan, northern Queens, and the South Bronx – saw the greatest improvement in air quality." What this data-dense press release conveys is that New Yorkers can thank the oil and gas industry's developments in the nearby Marcellus shale. The shale brings cleaner city air and healthier daily life.

Natural gas plays a large role in the U.S. economy, constituting 27% of total U.S. energy consumption in 2012.[60] Natural gas, unlike coal, is very flexible. It is used for generating electricity, powering some vehicles, providing heat to industry, commercial buildings, and homes as well as being a feedstock in the manufacture of hundreds of products like plastics and fertilizer. Its versatility elevates its value in our society.

Given the importance of natural gas in United States' energy portfolio, it is important to highlight the distinction between "wet" and "dry" natural gas. Wet gas is the natural gas that comes out of the ground from the drilling operations. This is before the gas is treated in any way. It is, essentially, raw and made up of methane molecules. However, wet gas also contains other valuable energy products that can add millions of dollars in revenue for companies involved in large drilling operations. These wet gas byproducts are called natural gas liquids (NGLs) and include ethane, propane, pentane, butane, and isobutane. On a chemical level, these molecules are all combinations of carbon atoms bound to varying numbers of hydrogen atoms. This raw, wet gas fuels several every day operations. We all know about the benefits of propane use in our barbecue grills and butane use for cigarette lighters. Ethane is a key NGL, however, due to its wide use as an industrial feedstock. Dry natural gas has had NGL's and other contaminates removed and is essentially the gas that is piped into our homes and businesses.

Some shale energy basins have natural gas production that contains very few NGLs; others, like the Marcellus Shale, are very rich in NGLs. These liquids are often quite valuable and enhance the shale energy production investment return; this is particularly important with regards to the current low natural gas prices. Furthermore, ethane is a major building block of plastics and other key chemical products. Due to the shale revolution, the United States now enjoys an abundant, low-priced supply of ethane. This ethane abundance has encouraged companies from around the world to invest billions in new United States' chemical and plastic manufacturing plants.

The Shale Revolution in Perspective:

The Bakken and Eagle Ford formations are estimated to have added more than 2 million barrels of oil production per day to the United States' oil output over just the past few years. One of the understandable challenges for lay people and media commentators is putting units, like millions of barrels per day, into a context that they can relate to in their everyday lives. The following example shows the value to our country's economy by increasing oil production by 2 million barrels per day and aligning that price figure up with some every day, ordinary items.

2,000,000 barrels of new shale oil production per day is equal to approximately $73 billion of revenue per year (2,000,000 BBLs x 365 days x $100 per barrel). Just to put this number in perspective, $73.0 billion is equal to each of the following:

- 2,920,000 cars (at $25,000 each), or
- 182,500 houses (at $400,000 each), or
- 127,845,888.4 shares of Google, Inc. Stock ($571.00 per share on July 10, 2014), or
- 730,000 boats (at $100,000 each), or
- 3,842,105 Harley Davidson, Inc. motorcycles (at $19,000 each), or
- 365,000 Ivy League college educations (at $200,000 each)

This 2 million barrels per day metric is, of course, just an example for the purpose of every day illustration. It does not include the massive daily gas production from the Marcellus shale, which can be converted to oil equivalents, or the production from other shale plays like the Permian.

Of course, total revenue or sales is not the amount that oil and gas companies retain from this increased production. Rather, the revenue figure becomes financial payments to hundreds of thousands of workers, steel suppliers, drilling contractors, landmen, engineers, state and local governments (as taxes), truck drivers, insurance companies, consultants, and thousands of other product and service suppliers.

The Challenges of Shale:

Shale energy, like all energy sources, has its challenges and problems. For example, there are several controversies surrounding hydraulic fracturing (discussed in Chapter 6), difficulty hiring sufficiently trained workers, rapid production decline rates, low natural gas prices, legal limitations on the export of oil from the United States, and high drilling costs. The list continues. Every day through these difficulties, the U.S. oil and gas industry still rises to the occasion and works to further enhance a booming, world-changing shale energy sector.

3
American Energy Innovation & Leadership

The future of the United States' energy sector will consist of an increasing number of important technological advances. Some of these new technologies will be revolutions or disruptions (as some people call them), and others will simply move our society forward to greater, solid ground. There will be a large group of key innovations, some evolutionary and some revolutionary. As a result, the competitive "playing field" between and among natural gas, solar, wind, oil, coal, and nuclear power in the United States will likely tilt back and forth a large number of times over the next 20-30 years. Sometimes these shifts will be significant. These potential shifts make it incredibly dangerous to declare an early technology winner in the battle for the United States' energy future. We are still in the first or 2nd inning of a 7 game play off. We're still stretching. We've hardly stepped up to the plate.

Fundamental Economic Structure:

We must understand the United States' energy sector's fundamental economic structure in order to fully appreciate the potential changes and potential impacts ahead in this imminent battle between shale and renewable energy sources. To begin, the energy sector is highly capital intensive. Economists use this term to mean that a business uses a lot of equipment and infrastructure in relation to the amount of labor that is used. The term "capital" includes any equipment, capital goods, and infrastructure used in finding and producing energy resources. This capital refers to the oil rigs, pipelines, steel pipe, etc. Of course, acquiring energy equipment and infrastructure requires large sums of money, which Wall Street and businesses also refer to as capital. In contrast to the energy sector, some businesses: law practices, investment banking, and insurance, for example, are relatively non-capital intensive. Capital intensity is important because the United States has trillions of dollars invested in our energy infrastructure (pipelines, refineries, thousands of drilling rigs, etc.). Our country will spend at least hundreds of billions more in the future decades in order to further innovation.

Another global energy industry characteristic lies in its large economies of scale. Having large economies of scale means that the cost per unit of output declines as total produced units rise. For example, petroleum refineries could be designed to easily just produce only 10,000 barrels of gasoline per day. Most refineries today, however, produce from 150,000 to 300,000 barrels of gasoline, jet fuel, or diesel per day in order to benefit from large economies of scale. Similarly, oil and gas drillers, nuclear power producers, offshore drilling rig operators, oil and gas pipeline companies, coal mining companies, and wind turbine manufacturers all strive to use advanced technologies to achieve ever increasing economies of scale. They work to drive per unit production costs as low as possible.

The history of economies of scale includes a leading American. John D. Rockefeller—a vilified monopolist—was perhaps not the best public relations practitioner. He was, however, one of the first oil men to recognize these economies of scale. With his insight as a starting point, Rockefeller formed and executed a strategy to aggressively acquire and consolidate refineries and pipeline operations in order to achieve significant operating scale for his company, Standard Oil. Standard Oil was the predecessor to Exxon, Mobil, Chevron, ARCO, and Amoco. ARCO and Amoco were acquired by British Petroleum; in later years, the company that brought the United States the largest oil spill in history.

The Marriage of Technology and Economics:

Technological innovation has a meaningful impact on the economics of the energy industry. The shale energy revolution is just the most recent example. Oil and gas industry technology breakthroughs are scaled up significantly and thereby lower costs for dozens of energy companies and millions of individual consumers.

Oil and gas detractors often pejoratively refer to the oil and gas industry as "big oil." This nickname has historical relevance: it is, perhaps a legacy of J.D. Rockefeller and his Standard Oil Trust, which was broken up by the federal government. Television commentators say grand things like: "Lobbyists are in the pockets of big oil" or "Big oil is out to destroy the environment." The truth is, the American people could pay incredibly higher prices from "small oil" energy. We need "big oil." It's not a fact we Americans always want to accept. This is because small companies are not able to reach the global oil companies' economies of scale.

The United States' energy industry has had a great many technology innovators over the past 200 years. These range from Colonel Edwin Drake who drilled the first oil well in America, Samuel Kier who was the first person to refine crude oil into kerosene, Thomas Edison who created the light bulb, Nikola Tesla who competed with Edison, and Fred C. Koch who invented catalytic cracking for refining crude oil. These were the great forbearers of the shale energy revolution.

Birth of the Shale Innovation:

However, much of the birth of the shale revolution can be attributed to one of the most important energy visionaries and innovators of the last 100 years: George Mitchell. Mitchell, who died on July 26, 2013 at 94, was the founder of Mitchell Energy, a Houston-based oil and gas company. Think of Steve Jobs and the personal computer. Think of Marc Andressen and the Internet. Mitchell was to shale energy what Steve Jobs and Marc Andressen were to technology. His contribution lies in igniting the world-changing shale revolution. An excellent tribute published in *The Economist* magazine on August 3, 2013 titled "Father of Fracking" asserts that "[f]ew business people have done as much to change the world as George Mitchell." Mitchell was born the son of Greek immigrants from Galveston, Texas. Through his strong education in petroleum engineering, hard work and tenacity, he went on to literally change the world.

The oil and gas industry innovations in shale production follow decades of innovation aimed to improve oil and gas exploration and production. Some of these technological innovations include: remotely operated vehicles (remote controlled submarines), deep water drilling (drilling thousands of feet below 3,000-6,000 feet of ocean), 3-dimensional and 4-dimensional seismic (a way of modeling and "seeing" underground oil reservoirs), catalytic cracking (a refining technique enabling more efficient refining of heavy oil), and SCADA systems (Supervisory Control and Data Acquisition, used for monitoring refineries, gas pipelines, the electric grid, etc.). Many petroleum industry innovations are necessary because of the harsh environments in which the industry operates. These environments include deserts, deep ocean water prone to hurricanes, and Alaskan frozen tundra. These are literally the most insane places to work; and yet America's oil and gas industry charges forward to meet the global desire for energy resources.

Additionally, other sectors of the economy lend their new technology to benefit the oil and gas industry; the oil and gas industry applies these techniques to their unique operational challenges. These adoptions include innovations and advancements from sectors in coatings, communications, filtration and fluids, health and environmental, inspection and monitoring, security, remote sensors, and a large number of software applications. Just like the medical technology and internet industries, for example, the oil and gas industry is constantly improving through relentless innovation.

Northern Ally Technology Innovations and Resources:

The Canadian oil sands sector also demonstrates the strategic importance of innovation within the oil and gas business; they've been innovating rapidly over the past 20 years. They've developed massive oil sands resources through advanced engineering, years of research, and billions of dollars in investment. The extraction of oil sands (technically, bitumen), which are also called "tar sands," initially required significant surface mining methods. These methods looked environmentally unfriendly and involved moving enormous amounts of earth with giant dump trucks and bulldozers. Essentially, their mining zone looked like a giant battlefield on Mars. It was a mess. Environmentalists were, justifiably, very concerned.

This earth-scraping, spaceman approach to mining the bitumen was necessary because oil sands exist in a semi-solid form rather than a liquid form like traditional crude oil. Therefore, the bitumen couldn't be produced through traditional oil drilling. Luckily, the oil and gas industry swooped in with further innovation: Steam Assisted Gravity Drainage (SAGD). This technology lowered the cost of extracting this heavy oil and significantly reduced the impact of its extraction on the environment. The Mars war was over. SAGD operations involved drilling a horizontal well rather than a vertical well. The horizontal well involves an initial vertical well drilled to a certain depth; then the drill bit turns 90 degrees and begins to drill horizontally beneath the underground bitumen formations. Steam is then injected through the well and into the formation below the oil sands. The steam rises up through the rocks and loosens the bitumen. The bitumen then flows down into a second well bore. The warm, liquid (but viscous) bitumen is then pumped to the surface.

These oil and gas operations highlight the benefit of oil and gas industry investments in research and innovation for Canada, the United States' largest oil supplier. Canada's oil sands resources amount to 170 billion barrels.[61] This places Canada third behind Venezuela and Saudi Arabia in total worldwide proved oil reserves.[62] The United States' politically stable ally to the north has the resources and the innovation to support us for decades.

Innovation Continuation:

Innovation is alive and well in every sector of the United States' energy industry, and it drives constant change. The shale energy revolution is an exciting event in our history, but it will not be the last major energy innovation the United States will enjoy. In a Forbes magazine article entitled 30 Under 30: Energy, the author, Christopher Helman, profiles 30 young leaders across the United States.[63] These brilliant innovators and entrepreneurs are making important contributions to our country's energy future.[64] The areas in which these young and innovative professionals are working include a smattering of projects including: improved aerodynamics for school buses, wellhead compression technology for natural gas wells, and electric vehicle chargers for devices that recharge electronics remotely using ultrasound transmitters. Further development lies in technology that converts carbon emissions into carbon nanotubes, an algae-based technology that turns the carbon dioxide that is emitted from cars into oxygen, new nuclear power technologies, and higher performance electric power transformers for light emitting diodes and consumer electronics and new nuclear reactors.[65] The list is broad; the people working endlessly are limitless. The point is this: the shale revolution is just one of many energy revolutions to come.

4

Myths & Reality:
The Oil and Gas Industry

Due to superficial news coverage, environmental hyperbole and some politicians who seek to demonize the industry, many Americans have a distorted view of our oil and gas industry.

<u>Myth:</u> The battle is really "Big Oil" vs. the American People.

<u>Reality:</u> We Americans need to change the way that we discuss the oil and gas industry. Lay people, politicians, news commentators, environmentalists, and political analysts discuss the oil and gas industry as though it exists on a remote island isolated from the rest of the United States. From this metaphorical island, it would seem that the oil industry regularly sets out on covert missions to inflict maximum damage on the rest of the United States in the form of "high" gasoline prices, massive oil spills, and general mayhem.

The truth is very different. Essentially, the American people are "Big Oil"—the very thing we proclaim to dislike or fear. The oil and gas industry employs hundreds of thousands of Americans and supports tens of thousands of small businesses. Think of your small, corner gas station, your local machine shops, consultants, trucking companies, water suppliers, excavators, accounting firms, transportation companies, etc.

Robert Shapiro and Nam D. Pham's 2011 study proclaims that 31.2% of the oil and gas industry is owned by individual investors while only 2.8% is owned by corporate management.[66] Therefore, Americans live well when America's oil and gas industry does well. We benefit from jobs, dividends and price appreciation in direct and indirect stocks. Direct stocks are ones we maintain ourselves and indirect stocks are ones we own through mutual funds and pensions. We live better from the oil and gas company tax payments as well. We benefit from our affluent quality of life; we have gasoline available to power our large SUV's, pickup trucks, boats, motorcycles, wave runners, lawn tractors and recreational vehicles.

Myth: Only a few big American oil companies control the industry.

Reality: The United States oil industry is made up of some big companies, including ExxonMobil, ConocoPhillips, Hess and Anadarko. Beyond these big companies, there are countless small independent oil and gas producers. These smaller companies compete with larger players like ExxonMobil by specializing in appropriate niches. These niches include specific drilling opportunities domestically and around the world. Mitchell Energy, for example, was once a small, independent oil and gas company that literally changed the world.

The real and very challenging concentration of power in oil and gas, which American oil companies of all sizes must battle, is held by numerous national oil companies around the world. National oil companies are those state-owned oil companies formed by national governments that control all of the oil and gas operations for an entire country. Among these are Saudi Aramco, Gazprom and Rosneft (majority owned by the Russian government), the National Iranian Oil Company, PetroChina, Pemex, Kuwait Petroleum, Abu Dhabi National Oil Company, Sonatrach (Algeria), Petrobras, Iraqi Oil Ministry, Petroleos de Venezuela, Qatar Petroleum and Statoil, among others.[67] National oil companies together control 70% of the world's oil reserves.[68] The 30% of world oil reserves that the national oil companies don't control or own is not what you might call the "low hanging fruit". These fields and drilling opportunities have been studied, explored and evaluated for decades and tend to be the higher-cost opportunities. For example, deep water wells in the Gulf of Mexico potentially hold billions of barrels of oil; however each field can cost billions to develop.

Myth: Oil and gas company CEO's are paid too much.

Reality: Oil Company Chief Executive Officers are paid well. Of course they are—you know that. Most CEO's in America are well paid, and deservedly so. Oil company CEO's run very large, complex organizations with global operations, and they have enormous responsibility to a large number of stakeholders. These stakeholders include: shareholders, tens of thousands of employees, governments, and local communities. They have a lot on their plates.

The real question involved in this myth, therefore, is the following: are oil company CEO's paid more than CEO's of comparably-sized organizations with similar geographic scope and complexity? A review of 2011 direct compensation data for sixteen of the world's largest oil companies (excluding national oil companies like Saudi Aramco) indicates that they are not overpaid. The average total direct CEO compensation in the study was $13.8 million: the largest the study found was ExxonMobil CEO's at $24.6 million a year while the lowest was Statoil ASA CEO at $1.7 million. (The companies reviewed were ExxonMobil, ConocoPhillips, Anadarko Petroleum, Chevron, Occidental, Marathon, Apache, BP, EOG Resources, Devon Energy, Hess, Royal Dutch Shell, Murphy Oil, Talisman Energy, Total S.A., and Statoil S.A.) (These figures do not include stock awards.) Obviously, these compensation levels are very high compared to the average worker; however, they are not dramatic compared to other CEO compensation levels across the United States.[69]

A look at the compensation data and analysis from the AFL-CIO lends great insight, as well. The AFL-CIO is a leading American labor union without staunch support for "big oil" management. The AFL-CIO published a list of the 100 highest compensated CEO's in the United States in 2012. This compensation did include stock and option awards so it is much more comprehensive. The highest paid CEO on the list was Larry Ellison of Oracle, at $96.0 million, while the "lowest" paid was Alexander Smith of Pier 1 Imports at $18.8 million.[70] Only 9 oil and gas companies were listed among the 100 companies: Exxon, Chevron, Cheniere, Occidental, Sandridge, Marathon, Anadarko, Conoco, and

Nabors. The average compensation for these 9 CEO's was $28.6 million, which is just slightly more than the list's median value of $25.1 million per year.[71] The CEO of Yahoo made $36.6 million—less than the CEO's of Cheniere and Exxon, but more than the CEO compensation of each of the other 7 oil companies listed above.[72]

Myth: The oil and gas industry makes huge profits.

Reality: This huge profit assertion is both true and untrue. Because of its large operations and economies of scale, the oil and gas industry generates large levels of revenue. These large revenues result in absolute levels of income or profits that can look enormous. Perhaps, to some observers, these levels of income could look unconscionable. If an oil company has $150 billion of sales and has a 10% net profit margin, for example, the profits of $15 billion can seem inordinately large. There is little evidence, however, that the oil and gas industry enjoys excessive profits. If it did, equity investors—your retired grandfather or the largest hedge fund—could readily and easily buy oil company stocks and share in the bounty. In today's environment, with thousands of mutual funds, electronically traded funds, and discount brokers, there are ample opportunities for millions of individuals to climb aboard the oil and gas profit train and thereby grow their retirement nest eggs.

Myth: The United States suffers from "high" gasoline prices.

Reality: Americans have made some interesting choices in relation to this myth. We drive SUV's and large pickup trucks, enjoy motor homes, purchase cars for our kids, and own millions of recreational boats. Although there is significant progress all the time to further usage of natural gas in truck and bus fleets across the United States, cars, SUVs and pickup trucks collectively boost consistent gasoline demand.

Also, due to chronic NIMBY ("not in my backyard") political opposition, a new oil refinery (with more than 100,000 barrel capacity) hasn't been built in the United States from the ground up in 37 years.[73] The last average-sized, complex refinery was built in 1977.[74] Think about this: the United States has more than 230 million cars, but there has not been a brand-new refinery built from the ground up since 1977—the first year of Jimmy Carter's presidency and the year Elvis Presley passed away. Although many existing refineries have been upgraded in these intervening years, the industry has had expansion inflexibility for decades. Think of this: for thirty-seven years, you've not been able to move forward, move out of your hometown, or really push yourself to the limits. This is similar to the factors inhibiting the oil and gas industry. More specifically, imagine present-day Intel Corporation or General Motors Corp. if they had not been able to build a new factory from the ground up since 1977. They would not have been able to seize the innovations they now hone.

Americans complain about "high" gasoline prices. It's an essential conversation: like talking about the weather. However, between driving large vehicles and constraining capacity growth through opposition to new refineries, we are actually contributing to high prices. Go figure.

Myth: Americans are energy gluttons.

Reality: The United States has 4.4% of the world's population (www.census.gov/popclock/) and consumes 20% of its petroleum.[75] This data can easily lead one to believe that Americans are energy gluttons. This, however, is not the case. The U.S. generates 23%-25% of the world's Gross Domestic Product: $16.6 trillion out of $54 trillion. This is basically the sum total of all of the products and services we make or provide in our own country. These numbers actually indicate that the American workforce is highly productive. Also, United States' energy intensity is consistently improving. Energy intensity is measured in BTU's per dollar of Gross Domestic Product. While GDP grew by 2.8% in 2012 to $16.6 trillion, total energy use fell by 2.4%. This resulted in a 5.1% decline in energy use per dollar of GDP.[76]

Myth: "Oil Barons" run the oil and gas industry:

Reality: "Oil Baron" is a term that works well in our age of bumper-sticker thinking and mass communication. But to what, precisely, does an oil baron refer? The petroleum industry detractors seek to draw a parallel between the post-civil war robber barons and today's oil industry executives. This characterization is inaccurate and burdensome. It forces inferior discussions about real energy industry issues. The robber barons of the mid-to-late 19th century in the United States were industrialists who exerted control over national resources, paid low wages, squashed competition by acquiring competitors before raising prices, and carried out schemes to sell stock at inflated prices.[77]

Therefore, utilizing the term "oil barons" allows petroleum industry opponents to "tar and feather" the oil and gas industry without defending their own positions with specific and logical arguments. Why don't we say "internet barons" or "grocery store barons" or "nursing home barons?" This name-calling perpetuates the myth of oil industry professionals as big, greedy, earth-destroying people. Hollywood has, of course, certainly done its share in perpetuating this characterization with movies like "Promised Land" and "There Will Be Blood."

Several oil and gas industry leaders disprove the "oil baron" characterization and its negative baggage. Of course we can look to the key hero of the shale energy boom: George Mitchell. Mitchell was a multi-billionaire when he passed away in 2013. However, rather than leaving all of his wealth to his family to create a sort of oil and gas dynasty, he joined other oil and gas industry billionaires by signing the Giving Pledge.

The Bill Gates and Warren Buffet-organized Giving Pledge is a commitment by a large number of billionaires to donate or will at least half of their fortunes to charity. Other oil and gas industry billionaires who have committed to the Giving Pledge are Harold Hamm, the CEO of Continental Resources, an important developer in the Bakken oil play, T. Boone Pickens, the natural gas legend and head of his own hedge fund, and David Rockefeller, the grandson of John D. Rockefeller.

Myth: The United States' oil and gas industry profits from "subsidies":

Reality: This claim actually falls into two general categories: tax "breaks" and military spending to protect Middle East sources of oil.

Much of the controversy around oil and gas industry tax breaks or "subsidies" has to do with two tax benefits:

1) The expensing rather than the capitalization (like depreciation) of intangible drilling costs.
2) The deduction of a percentage of the oil and gas produced each year under the "percentage of completion" method for oil and gas wells.

Intangible drilling costs may sound inconceivable—like they were invented at Enron. However, these costs are very real and include expenses relating to preparation of an oil field for production. These expenses include site preparation, clearing, excavation, surveys, fuel, etc. Allowance for oil companies to subsidize these costs has been around for 100 years. The original idea understood that drilling an oil well was very risky; expensing these costs helped drillers increase their investment returns and attracted additional capital to the oil and gas industry.

The percentage of depletion tax credit essentially allows some oil and gas companies to take a tax deduction equal to a percentage of their oil and gas revenues. This is because oil and gas reserves require a lot of capital investment; they are a wasting asset, just like factory machinery or construction equipment in other industries. Their equipment and site will depreciate over time.

A recent Forbes magazine article about oil and gas industry subsidies began with the following interesting quote:

"Now my recollection of what a subsidy means is when you are given money to do something. I guess when I drilled 17 dry holes in a row I missed that pay window. No one sent me a check." –

Harold Hamm, Chairman and CEO of Continental Resources[78]

One could promote a good strategy for the oil and gas industry to support a partial-repeal of these controversial tax deductions. This could promote better relations with the public. According to a May 2012 study by the Congressional Research Service, these two tax deductions will cost taxpayers $25 billion between 2013 and 2022. That is an average of $2.5 billion per year. A 50% reduction in these tax breaks would cost the oil and gas industry $1.25 billion per year; of course the industry could afford this cost.

There are, however, two problems with this strategy. As soon as the oil and gas industry agrees to a 50% reduction, all of the anti-oil factions in the media, Congress, and among environmentalist organizations would immediately demand 100% elimination of the credits. Furthermore, the oil and gas industry is continually volatile. Any number of plausible scenarios could lead to lower oil and/or gas prices in the coming years, thus reducing the sectors profitability.

The second major issue regarding oil and gas industry "subsidies" involves the U.S. military and our country's defense of certain "allies" in the Middle East. The United States' billions of dollars of aid to Israel, Egypt, Saudi Arabia, and the war in Iraq are partially used for the purpose of keeping oil supplies readily available for Americans. When these funds were first utilized, this was a responsible strategy by United States' government. It allowed avoidance of a repeat of the OPEC infliction of oil embargoes of the 1970's.

However, this strategy did not benefit the oil and gas industry; it was meant to protect American consumers and businesses. Had Iran, for example, been able to take over Saudi Arabia and its oil fields sometime over the past 30 years, oil prices would have skyrocketed. U.S. oil and gas companies would have received an enormous windfall. Therefore, the United States' military presence in the Middle East benefited the oil industry only to the extent that it ensured fairly stable prices. Remarkably, the shale revolution is decreasing the need for OPEC oil and its biggest producer, Saudi Arabia.

In summary, all of these myths are old baggage that only serves to stand in the way of further American oil and gas industry innovation.

5

New Jobs and Manufacturing

New Job Creation:

Since the onset of the 2009 Great Recession, the shale oil and gas revolution has generated tens of thousands of new jobs. Furthermore, the shale boom has pulled the economic center of activity from the east and west coasts of the United States to the middle of the country— bringing massive wealth to the states needing a real boost. Wall Street, the entertainment industry of the Los Angeles area, and the Silicon Valley internet and technology sectors no longer maintain domination of the economy. The shale revolution focuses in Texas, North Dakota, Pennsylvania, Ohio, etc., in many ways the heart of America.

This wealth-shift is found easily in Pennsylvania, home of the enormous Marcellus shale play. Because of the Marcellus play, the natural gas industry is partnering with two-year colleges to establish programs that will train students to work in the natural gas industry— thus pushing new job opportunities into the area. The Pittsburgh Technical Institute opened a new $3.5 million Energy Technology Center in October of 2013.[79] This is an innovative center focused on teaching young people how to test and maintain and repair oilfield electronics.

The shale revolution is keeping the wealth in-country. The jobs the shale revolution creates are not outsourced to China or India like the computer programming or customer service center jobs of past

41

decades. These shale-related positions are local jobs focused on delivering steel pipe, pipeline welding, pouring concrete, creating and delivering gravel, excavation services, supplying water, etc. These services create stable, secure middle-class jobs across the U.S. They work toward a better middle class for people seeking to put their kids through college and maintain a decent retirement.

Furthermore, landowners like farmers and ranchers generate lease income from energy companies seeking drilling space on their land. Many are becoming what the CBS News "60 Minutes" television show recently referred to as "Shalionaires." The income they sustain comes in the form of bonuses, lease payments, and possible royalties (if a well is ultimately drilled on their land and energy is produced). These payments typically go back to the local economy to support local business growth.

A recent article by Conglin Xu of the Oil and Gas Journal (9/5/2013) summarized the following findings from an IHS Inc. report entitled "America's New Energy Future: The Unconventional Oil & Gas Revolution & the U.S. Economy, Vol. 3." According to the report:

- "Unconventional energy increased U.S. household disposable income by $1,200 in 2012, [will] approach $2,000 in 2015, and $3,500 in 2025 due to reduced costs of energy and other goods and services."
- "During 2012-25, IHS projects a total of more than $2.4 trillion will be invested in the upstream oil and gas activities. Midstream and downstream energy will generate about $216 billion and energy-related chemicals will add more than $129 billion."
- "Unconventional oil and gas activity and employment contributed a total of more than $74 billion in government revenues in 2012"

The Manufacturing Sector:

The United States' chemicals manufacturing sector is reaping tremendous benefits from the shale revolution. The future outlook for relatively low natural gas prices in the United States has spurred new investments in national chemical plants.

According to a May 2013 study released by the American Chemistry Council:

"$71.7 billion in chemical industry investments (97 projects) to build and/or expand in the U.S. will generate 485,000 jobs in construction and capital goods manufacturing, i.e., process equipment, tanks, pipes, valves, etc. The $71.7 billion in announced chemical industry investments will lead to $66.8 billion in increased chemical industry output. This is a 9% gain above what output would otherwise be in 2020. The $66.8 billion in new chemical industry output will require more chemical industry workers, creating more than 46,000 direct chemical industry jobs."[80]

The United States has lost tens of thousands of manufacturing jobs over the past twenty or thirty years. Many of these high value jobs were in automobile manufacturing, steel production, and furniture. For obvious manufacturing reasons, energy is a major cost component of millions of products. Therefore, high energy prices here in the United States raise our cost of production and make our products less competitive.

The industrial sector of manufacturing, mining, agriculture, and construction accounted for almost a third of total 2012 U.S. energy use.[81] For example, the cement sector is a huge energy consumer. Consider the thousands of buildings built with concrete every year. Although the cement industry uses only one-quarter of one percent of total U.S. energy, it is the most energy-intensive of all manufacturing industries. Its share of national energy use is roughly 10 times its share of the nation's gross output of goods and services.[82] 10 times its share of gross output is an incredible amount. Other energy intensive industries like steel, aluminum, bulk chemicals, and paper products have a share of energy use at an average of roughly twice their share of gross output.[83]

What does all of this mean for our state, regional and national economy? The shale energy revolution has lowered the cost structure of millions of businesses across the country. For example, consider the thousands of companies that supply products to the big three U.S. car manufacturers and the foreign manufacturing factories. The United States automobile industry produced 11.1 million cars and light trucks in 2013.[84] The benefit of these lower energy and product costs will accrue to future United States' workers and consumers.

6

Hydraulic Fracturing: Innovation or Public Relations Nightmare?

Hydraulic fracturing, the well-tested and widely used method of stimulating oil and gas production in a tight reservoir, is now commonly referred to, often pejoratively, as "fracking". Fracking is a very unfortunate name—perhaps something alluding to a medieval method of torture. A medieval English king could command: "Let's start fracking the prisoner right away!" or "He needs to be fracked twice before we lop off his head!" Of course, "fracking" is shorter and punchier than saying the drawn-out words "hydraulic fracturing," particularly when conceiving alarming, bumper-sticker style headlines. Every newspaper needs a catchy title.

The Truth and the History:

Environmental alarmists spout the evils of hydraulic fracturing. However, the truth about hydraulic fracturing is incredibly mundane. Hydraulic fracturing has been used to enhance oil well production since the late 1940's. The past 65 to 70 years have brought hydraulic fracturing to more than 1,000,000 United States oil and gas wells. Hydraulically fractured wells amount to perhaps as many as 2.5 million worldwide, as well.[85] Furthermore, these 1 million hydraulically fractured wells in the United States equate to an average of approximately 15,386 wells per year over approximately 65 years. Clearly, the oil and gas industry wouldn't get away with hydraulically fracturing

1,276 wells (on average) every month for 65 years in a row if the practice were dangerous or environmentally harmful.

Hydraulic fracturing technology evolved from the late 1940's to around the year 2000. The subsequent Mitchell Energy innovations improved hydraulic fracturing's work in shale rock formations. The Mitchell Energy approach to a well-tested (no pun intended) technology, however, did not involve a fundamental change in well drilling through the vertical portion of horizontal wells. Therefore, the drill bits pass through underground well water supplies just like the drilling involved with conventional oil and gas wells. This is because water supplies are typically located in relatively shallow aquifers and the oil which we seek lies below the water supply. Therefore, the actual hydraulic fracturing occurs far below the fresh water aquifers. Yes, the wells are drilled through the water supply. However, this has been the drilling well procedure for more than 100 years. The steel pipe and cement casing around each bore hole in the well provide immense protection against mud leaks (drilling fluid) and hydraulic fracturing fluid leaks in the water supply.

The Environmental War:

Environmentalists have declared war on hydraulic fracturing. They declared war in spite of the many shale energy economic and environmental benefits. These benefits enhance natural gas' competition against renewable energy in this age when environmentalists are working constantly for renewable energy resources. One group, Americans Against Fracking, is an umbrella group made up of 100+ organizations.[86] These organizations include 350.org, Climate Mama, MoveOn.org, Friends of the Earth, Environmental Action, Rainforest Action Network, Progressive Democrats of America, Greenpeace, Water Keeper Alliance, and Oil Change International.

Truthland, a documentary rebuttal to Josh Fox's anti-fracking documentary *Gasland*, features the Director of the Environmental Defense Fund's acknowledgement that fracking is not his primary concern with respect to the shale gas drilling "dangers." (Watch the documentary

Truthland on Youtube.com. Find his comments around 16 minutes and 59 seconds into the documentary.)

Note: If you are interested in learning more about hydraulic fracturing chemical-use, look to the web site www.fracfocus.org. As of mid-June 2014, the site had information on the chemicals used to hydraulically fracture 72,735 oil and gas wells.

Artists and Actors Attack the Industry:

We should have an honest debate about the perceived and actual dangers of hydraulic fracturing. It is, as Americans, our right to discuss our own opinions about the country around us. Unfortunately, the strongest opinions and loudest voices are often found in Hollywood actors. It is difficult to imagine more unqualified individuals. As Americans, these actors have every right to speak out on any subject they wish. Because these actors are famous, however, the media lends them great attention. These actors are, of course, well intentioned; we all want clean and safe water. But do these actors add any real insight or valuable analysis for the benefit of policymakers and voters who must decide hydraulic fracturing allowances and regulations?

Artists Against Fracking, for example, is a group of talented actors and musicians against hydraulic fracturing in New York. It is very prominent: Yoko Ono and Sean Lennon (John's son) were the forefathers; their website lists Alec Baldwin, Mark Ruffalo, Susan Sarandon, Richard Gere, Jimmy Fallon, and many other prominent entertainers, as members.[87] We can assume their intentions are good. However, they are not qualified to judge the safety of hydraulic fracturing. One of the group's central contributions is a video called "Don't Frack My Mother."[88] Their conclusions are unverified. We require highly qualified physicists, chemical engineers, biologists, medical researchers, and geologists to render the safety issue. This country requires a balanced, well-reasoned approach to hydraulic fracturing—without the theatrics and hyperbole. You don't listen to your three year old about whether or not preschool is necessary or not. Your three year old has no understanding of the greater world.

Of course, very wealthy entertainers fighting shale energy promotes incredible irony. These artists are likely part of the top 1% of United States' highest income earners; other activist organizations rail against this 1% on a regular basis. They fly around the United States in private planes and boast expensive natural gas heated houses that bring resources from fracking-legalized Pennsylvania. Is this anti-fracking activism nothing more than the top 1% of wealth holders telling the bottom 99% that cheap energy and well-paying middle class oil and gas jobs should not be available to the average American?

Perhaps an alternative way for artists (actors and musicians) to contribute to the issue of hydraulic fracturing safety would be for wealthy artists to do the following:

1. Form a trust fund or foundation for the purpose of funding research on hydraulic fracturing.
2. Hire a group of highly credible, non-partisan trustees.
3. Collect a $1 million dollar donation from 100 wealthy actors, musicians, painters, etc.
4. Hire the best chemists, physicists, medical researchers, drilling engineers and petroleum geologists (from leading universities, if the goal is independence).
5. Conduct peer-reviewed research.
6. Publish findings on the trust fund's or foundation's website and invite comments from the public and policy makers.
7. Create a documentary laying out the qualifications of the researchers and the facts underlying the conclusions arrived at.

United States' Environmental Protection Agency:

The United States' Environmental Protection Agency (EPA) is a critically important arbiter in this hydraulic fracking environmental debate. The EPA creates responsible studies focused on the fracking shale oil and gas issues. According to the EPA: "In response to public concern, the U.S. House of Representatives requested that the U.S.

Environmental Protection Agency conduct scientific research to examine the relationship between hydraulic fracturing and drinking water resources (USHR, 2009)."[89] In 2011, the EPA began research under its "Plan to Study the Potential Impacts of Hydraulic Fracturing on Drinking Water Resources." The study's purpose is to assess the potential impacts of hydraulic fracturing on drinking water resources and to identify the driving factors that may affect the severity and frequency of such impacts. Scientists focus primarily on studies including hydraulic fracturing of natural gas in shale formations; they promote further study of other oil and gas-producing formations, including tight sands and coalbeds."[90] This study by the EPA is scheduled for completion sometime in late 2014.

A key test of the hydraulic fracturing politics is currently on display in New York State. Environmentalists hope that a key victory against hydraulic fracturing in New York will reverse their losses in many other states that now allow hydraulic fracturing. New York hydraulic fracturing has been delayed since 2008. That year, the New York Department of Environmental Conservation began an extensive review of hydraulic fracturing; New York State Department of Health is now evaluating that review. The key issue is to address any hydraulic fracturing environmental and health concerns before Governor Cuomo makes his final hydraulic fracturing ruling to deny or grant permission.[91]

Many observers and energy industry participants are frustrated with Governor Cuomo's Administration for delaying this decision for more than 5 years. These frustrated observers include New York landowners who could benefit from drilling operation land leases. The Joint Landowners Coalition of New York is in the process of bringing a lawsuit against the State; they seek to force the Cuomo Administration to make a fracking decision.[92] They argue that their fundamental property rights are denied because they are unable to lease their land to oil and gas companies.

Governor Cuomo is facing reelection in November 2014, and he feels the pressure: from both anti-fracking and pro-fracking groups. When asked in mid-November 2013 whether he expected a decision on hydraulic fracturing by Election Day, 2014, Cuomo affirmed there would be a decision.[93] His political motives prompt Governor Cuomo to delay this decision. The delay allows him flexibility if new information is revealed that argues strongly in favor or against hydraulic fracturing. For the hundreds of landowners that could benefit from hydraulic fracturing and the thousands of recipients of new fracking-related jobs, however, another year is a long time to wait.

Many states have already approved hydraulic fracturing. Even California, a clear leader on clean and renewable energy, is implementing stringent regulations that allow hydraulic fracturing. California Democratic Governor Jerry Brown released draft regulations permitting fracking that are consistent with a 2012 California legislative bill.[94] These regulations go into effect in 2015; however, fracking was permitted to begin on emergency-basis after January 1, 2014.[95] Furthermore, the Illinois' Department of Natural Resources issued proposed regulations that permit hydraulic fracturing.[96] While Cuomo Administration continues to drag its heels, the rest of the country is charging forward with the shale revolution.

However, on June 30, 2014, the Court of Appeals, New York State's highest court, ruled that local towns and cities can establish and impose bans on oil and gas operations within their jurisdictions.[97] These local bans were deemed by the high court to be extensions of local zoning laws rather than being rules that would regulate the specific operations and procedures related to oil and gas operations. Anti-fracking activists hope that communities around the United States will be able to impede the growth of hydraulic fracturing by imposing similar local ordinances and arguing that they are also natural extensions of each town's local zoning ordinances.

Notwithstanding this victory in New York State, it is highly uncertain whether this legal strategy can be implemented successfully by anti-fracking activists on a widespread basis across the United States. State laws, of course, vary and hundreds of communities across Texas, North Dakota, Pennsylvania and other states have reaped enormous economic benefits from hydraulic drilling activities.

7

OPEC: A Slow, Painful Decline

Middle Eastern countries Iraq, Iran, Kuwait, Saudi Arabia, and Venezuela formed the Organization of the Petroleum Exporting Countries (OPEC) in 1960.[98] Since this dramatic formation, OPEC has been a gorilla with its hands wrapped around the world's oil pipeline. Thankfully, due to the shale oil revolution, this giant gorilla is unstable and losing its grip on that pipeline. Let's look at the numbers: in 2012, the United States imported 4.27 million BBLs per day from OPEC. These imports cost $427 million per day (assuming $100 per barrel for the price of oil), a combined 2012 total of $155.9 billion. Essentially, every American man, woman and child (population 317 million) sent OPEC approximately $491.00.

OPEC History:

Americans knew little about OPEC until its October 1973 Arab oil embargo against the United States. They did this to retaliate against the United States' support of Israel. This created the United States' first oil shock. This was the era of the Watergate scandal; in less than a year, Richard Nixon would become the first President of the United States to resign. In that year, oil prices quadrupled, and gasoline was rationed. To make matters worse, the United States experienced decreased domestic oil production after its peak was reached in 1970.

OPEC Today:

OPEC, while weaker, is certainly not dead yet. It will continue in the short and intermediate term to impact oil prices. Oil price trends will be critically important to the ongoing growth of production of shale oil in the United States. Unlike the natural gas market, which is just now becoming part of a global market, U.S. oil prices are highly dependent on global prices. In other words, there is a single, global market for oil. Declining global oil prices could quickly bring a halt to a meaningful portion of U.S. oil production. Saudi Arabia and many of the other members of OPEC have much lower production costs than those in the shale plays of the United States. It is unlikely that key member countries within OPEC will sit back and continue to lose market share to U.S. shale oil. It would not be surprising to see OPEC adopt a deliberate strategy of driving down oil prices to the low to mid $80 dollar per barrel range to drive marginal American producers out of the market.

OPEC's flexibility in reducing pricing, however, should not be overstated. Many of OPEC's leading oil producing countries, including Saudi Arabia, have very large domestic social program costs that must continue to be funded. These governments (Arab, Persian and others) have carefully watched the widespread toppling of governments during the Arab Spring. The governments in Tunisia, Libya and Egypt have all fallen, and a devastating civil war continues to be fought in Syria. Iran is now facing crippling sanctions because of its nuclear program and Iraq is returning only slowly to full historical oil production. Saudi Arabia is particularly sensitive to internal threats to its regime and any potential increased threat from Iran, which seems to be ever closer to having nuclear bomb technology (if not the ability to weaponize it).

OPEC and Domestic Social Problems:

Potentially lower future oil prices, not caused by new policies from OPEC but, instead, due to increased oil production in new shale oil resources across America could have a destabilizing effect on some of these key OPEC producers. Measuring the cost of production for each OPEC nation versus the current price of oil (for example, $100/BBL for oil and $20 per barrel for production costs) tells only a small part of the story of OPEC's oil economics. More important is the net revenue from oil that must be spent on massive domestic social programs to keep the citizens of OPEC countries from rising up and toppling their governments. If the breakeven price for OPEC supplied crude is defined as the oil price necessary to have a balanced fiscal budget for each country in the cartel (rather than oil price less cost of production), then many countries are close to or even below breakeven.

APICORP published an analysis of these breakeven costs in the Middle East Economic Survey in August 2012. Their analysis provides a "fiscal budget break even" point for each of the major oil producing countries in the Middle East.[99] The social spending break even points ranged from $53.00 per BBL for Qatar to $127.00 per BBL for Iran. Saudi Arabia's breakeven point was estimated to be $94.00 per BBL.[100] Saudi Arabia came in a bit below the average of $99.00 per BBL for all OPEC members.[101] This analysis suggests that if OPEC members want to continue their social spending and avoid fiscal deficits, oil prices must remain around $100 per BBL. Brent crude oil sells at around $110 per BBL as of late May 2014, allowing OPEC's revenues (approximately $100 per BBL x 30.1 million barrels per day is $3 billion per day or $1.1 trillion per annum) to stand where they must to avoid painful social spending cutbacks.[102]

In 2012, American "ally" Saudi Arabia earned about $311 billion revenue from total global oil sales. Saudi Arabia sold the United States 1.365 million BBLs of oil per day and collected annual revenues of about $49.8 billion. Note: all of these calculations assume a $100 per barrel price.[103]

Import Decrease in Exchange for American Oil:

But there is good news. The United States oil imports from OPEC decreased from 2007 to 2012: down 28.6% from 5.98 million BBLs per day to 4.27 million BBLs per day.[104] Nigeria's United States' oil sales dropped dramatically.[105] United States' Nigerian imports fell 61% from 1.13 million barrels per day to 441,000 barrels per day in 2012.[106] This reduction is the result of rapid oil production increases in the Bakken, Eagle Ford, and Permian shale plays. New shale oil production from the Bakken and Eagle Ford formation is displacing crude oil from Mexico, Venezuela, and Saudi Arabia. After spending the past 40 years under OPEC's thumb, this is a welcome relief.

The relief, in numbers, is staggering. The United States has spent $5 trillion on OPEC crude oil imports since 1970 (in constant 2008 dollars).[107] Much of this $5 trillion would have been spent on foreign oil supplies even if OPEC had not existed. America did not have the domestic oil production available to feed our huge economic engine. Accurate estimates of oil's free market price are difficult to create; therefore, it's impossible to calculate the United States' overpayment due to OPEC's control of the global oil market (what economists call an oligopoly). For the sake of argument, however, let's suppose that $1.5 trillion dollars of this $5 trillion total represents an "overpayment" for OPEC oil.

$1.5 trillion dollars. Wow. What could the United States have invested this money in instead? The table below relates a rough estimate of how much general and energy infrastructure could be developed with this assumed $1.5 trillion:

Hypothetical Alternative Uses of Capital Sent to OPEC: Table 7-1

Infrastructure	Quantity	Assumed Cost (each)	Total Cost
New High Schools	10,000	$100 million	$1.0 trillion
New Home Furnaces	26,000,000	$10,000	$0.265 trillion
3 MW Wind Turbines	30,000	$1.21 million / MW	$0.11 trillion
Refineries	20	$5 billion	$0.1 trillion
Natural Gas Pipelines (36 inches)	5,000 miles	$138,889 per inch mile(1)	$0.025 trillion
Total			**$1.5 trillion**

Source: Hypothetical scenario. Costs are assumed. 1) An inch- mile means that one mile of 36 inch pipeline would cost 36 x $138,889.89 or $5.0 million per mile.

Estimated amounts in the table above show that the potential for United States infrastructure without the existence of OPEC is quite extensive. These numbers are difficult to quantify. Sending billions of dollars per day ("petrodollars") to OPEC over the last 40 years, however, required a lot of money that could have been put to good use here in United States. About this, there should be little dispute.

8

Energy Prices: The Wildcard

"How much does it cost?" is the ever-resounding question in our lives. And the same is true in the natural gas, oil, and renewable energy sectors. The crux of the battle between shale and renewable energy is price competition. This price competition is based on natural gas' electricity production versus electricity production from renewable sources like wind, hydro and, solar power. The battle, however, is somewhat asymmetrical: natural gas replaces wind and solar more easily than wind and solar replace natural gas.

Price Outlook: United States' Energy Understanding Lacks Complete Historical Context:

Some lay people and media analysts in the United States often tend to mistakenly take the most recent 3 years of experience, whether low prices or declining demand or pipeline bottlenecks, and extrapolate this limited experience for years or decades into the future. For example, in the early 1980's many analysts and commentators said that oil prices would continue to rise indefinitely (they crashed in late 1985 thanks to Saudi Arabia flooding the market). Also, in the mid-to-late 1980's the gas bubble (or chronic oversupply) caused by the Fuel Use Act was thought to mean that natural gas prices would stay low for many years to come (prices came back up in the early 1990's, partially due to the repeal of the Act).

In 2005, the threat of "peak oil" caused some economists to believe that oil was charging toward $300 per barrel and that the United States would need to import LNG supplies of natural gas. Partially due to this scare, oil prices actually rose to $145 per BBL in July 2008. [108]

Of course, conventional oil and gas reserves are increasingly difficult and expensive to discover and develop. After 100 plus years of global oil and gas exploration, all the elephants (giant oil or gas fields) are discovered; "low hanging fruit" no longer exist in the conventional oil and gas sector. The conventional boom is over. Without the shale oil boom, the global oil price would be significantly higher than the $100-$110 per barrel price that prevailed as of late May 2014.

Volatile Gas Prices:

Over the past 20 years or more, natural gas prices in the United States have been quite volatile. This is primarily due to the bottlenecks in the natural gas pipeline network and frequent instances of sharply increased demand caused by unusually cold weather in the Northeast and the upper Midwest

The future may bring stability. The United States finds more abundant supplies scattered geographically around the country, taking the vast distance of pipeline transportation out of the equation. Shale gas claims closer proximity to major consuming markets. For example, the huge Marcellus shale area is much closer to the great metropolitan areas of Philadelphia, Pittsburgh, New York City, and Boston than gas fields located in Louisiana, Texas, and Oklahoma.

Gas and Oil Prices: The Truth Behind the Prices

Natural gas prices seem inexplicable. However, logic exists behind the numbers. Natural gas prices depend on several things including: commercial transactions among consumers and producers, over-the-counter traders, companies seeking to hedge their exposures to gas price volatility, speculators, and traders on the futures exchanges. Natural gas has a very large domestic and international commodity market; its forward prices (natural gas future delivery prices) are available on the futures market for 18-24 months into the future, with varying degrees of liquidity.

Ultimately, the widening gap between natural gas price and oil price per million BTU's has affected the United States' past years' oil and natural gas prices. In other words, we need to compare oil and gas prices on an "apples-to-apples" basis. The energy content of a barrel of oil is approximately 6 million BTU's versus gas' content of about 1 million BTU's per MCF. In theory, then, oil prices should be close to 6 times the price of natural gas. Because oil and natural gas are not perfect substitutes for each other, however, the 6(x) ratio can be somewhat higher or lower at different times.

April 2014, however, brought natural gas prices to around $5 per mm BTU's while oil prices were around $100 per barrel. Applying the 6(x) ratio of oil to gas prices suggests that oil prices should be $30 per barrel (6x gas prices of $5 is $30). Alternatively, dividing the $100 per BBL oil price by 6 suggests that natural gas prices should be $16 per mm BTU's. The ratio of crude oil to natural gas prices is now about 20:1, instead of the aforementioned 6:1. This current 20:1 ratio reflects the ramp-up of natural gas production from the shale oil boom in recent years and the resulting decline of gas prices. Think of it this way: we can only relate something's price based on its availability. Natural gas is hugely abundant. It's currently like the McDonald's of energy resources.

This skewed price relationship between natural gas and oil developed over the past few years is likely to continue. However, equilibrium is likely to be found. By 2020, natural gas exports through pipelines and liquefied natural gas terminals could bridge the gap between oil and gas prices (i.e. 6x price ratio). However, the next 5-10 years' outlook suggests that heating oil consumers will switch to natural gas for economic reasons. The best candidates for conversion are companies that operate fleets of vehicles. Think of UPS and Federal Express, for example; they are increasing their compressed natural gas use to power their vehicles.

Hydraulic fracturing drives shale oil production across the United States; however, oil prices play a key role in shale oil production, as well. Lower oil prices offer a key risk in the oil and gas industry. Drilling for shale oil entails fairly high costs—costs that must be met via a certain oil price. Drilling rigs are in demand, steel prices are creeping up, and there is keen competition for talent. Land lease costs for major shale plays have increased dramatically, as well.

Energy commodity prices are notoriously difficult to predict. The prices are affected by a large number of variables including weather, pipeline capacity, oil and gas storage availability, demand for competing fuels, electric utility production capacity changes, automobile fuel economy, regulatory changes, and limits on carbon emissions. For example: the great winters of the northeast United States are unpredictable and force the commodity demand to increase. This demand creates a greater price.

The recent period of low and stable natural gas prices will not continue; the wide gap between oil and gas prices is not constant. This future uncertainty is one of the key reasons why the competitive battle between conventional energy and renewable energy is far from settled.

9

Energy Security or Independence?

The average American may not understand two key and very different concepts: energy security and energy independence. And the confusion and lack of knowledge is expected. The media reports on the energy sector through sound bites and two-minute supposed-analyst reports. The information is lacking and unclear. Let's break these two key points down.

Energy Independence:

Because of America's likely continued significant consumption of crude oil (from both shale and conventional sources), we may not have significantly more energy independence in the years to come than we have in years past. What many news and internet commentators and others not actively involved in the energy industry sometimes fail to understand is that crude oil is traded on the global market. Global oil prices respond almost instantaneously (thanks to the internet and 24/7 news coverage) to changes in global oil and gas demand and supply. Essentially, a large political or economic shock elsewhere in the world could cause a sharp spike in oil prices and have a large impact on the American economy.

For example, suppose that the United States produced all of its own oil in the year 2025 (not a prediction, just a supposition) and war broke out between Iran and China. Assume in this scenario that Iran is a nuclear power by 2025. In order to get a chokehold on China's economy which imports significant amounts of oil every year, Iran invades Saudi Arabia and topples the government. Oil prices spike overnight from $150 per barrel to $400 per barrel once the news is reported. American oil production and supplies are then re-priced to reflect the cost of importing oil. Effectively, the new price of oil in America would become $400 in a matter of hours. Americans would have to pay $8-$10 per gallon for gasoline. Therefore, even if the United States becomes self sufficient in the production of oil, we will remain vulnerable to price shocks caused by the political, military, and economic events around the world.

Energy Security:

The United States finally revels in energy security. After Americans watched the past eight presidents call a national initiative to gain energy security, the private oil and gas sector put the United States on the path to energy security. They developed massive shale oil and gas resources. Therefore, we no longer have such an import need. History shows the scary trajectory of imports in the United States: oil imports rose steadily from the 1970's through the early 2000's and reached a high of 60% in 2005.[109] The shale oil production advances allowed imports of oil (crude and petroleum products) to decline to 40% in 2012.[110]

As quoted on the issue of "energy independence" in a Forbes Magazine article published December 10, 2012, Richard Kinder, Chairman of Kinder Morgan, made the following observation:

"If people think we can draw a circle around North America and that we can be an independent island of energy, that's not realistic. This is a world market for oil, for refined products and increasingly for natural gas."

While the United States has enjoyed incredible success in increasing oil production, the Obama Administration continues to push reduction of transportation-used gasoline. They want to enhance energy security by increasing the manufacture and sale of electric-powered cars and light trucks. Electric car producer Tesla has met tremendous success in addressing a small, niche market; other car manufacturers are increasing their electric car offerings. For example, Nissan and General Motors have had their Leaf and Volt car models in the marketplace for the past few years.

CAFÉ Standards:

CAFE standards, or Corporate Average Fuel Economy Standards, force a reduction of domestic oil consumption. These standards, which were first passed by Congress in 1975, require car companies to produce cars with a specific average fuel economy. On August 28, 2013, however, the Obama Administration announced that it will implement a new set of CAFE standards that require average fuel economy of 54.5 miles per gallon by 2025.[111] Existing standards require average fuel economy to reach the equivalent of 35.5 miles per gallon by 2016.[112]

A Note on Electric Vehicles:

Electric cars could reduce greenhouse gas emissions if the produced electric power comes from clean energy sources like natural gas, wind, or solar—not coal or oil. You don't want to fill up your electric vehicle with electricity generated from greenhouse-gas-spewing coal. That would really miss the point.

Beyond the successful Tesla Motors, however, the electric car market is still in its infancy. Hybrid cars have held fair success in serving a niche market. The infancy remains as the general public cannot adopt with the limited range of electric cars and their relative high costs. Further, many require that homeowners buy special charging equipment for their homes that can cost $1,000 to $4,000.

During all of 2013, United States' sales of plug-in automobiles (hybrids, electrics, etc.) totaled 592,232 or 3.8% of the 15.5 million new cars sold during the same period.[113] This market share is up from the 2.23% and 3.38% achieved in 2011 and 2012, respectively.[114] Clearly, the plug-in car is still a niche market. However, the costs of plug-in cars will likely decline over time as mass-market buyers replace these early adopters.

A growing area of new vehicle technology lies in electric-powered motorcycles. These vehicles could provide economic transportation to millions of people. A number of new and innovative companies in the United States are developing and marketing new electric motorcycle models. By nature of their design, motorcycles enjoy high power-to-weight ratios (horsepower per vehicle pound) compared to heavy, five-passenger cars. Therefore, electric motorcycles generally have better relative ranges (distance that can be driven on a single electric charge) than electric cars.

Let's take a moment to understand range and why it's important. For example, a gasoline powered car might have a range of 360 miles (assume a 12 gallon gas tank and a fuel economy of 30 miles per gallon) while an electric car might only have a 70 mile range between electric charges. Therefore, an electric car's range is about 20% of the conventional car's range (70/360 or 19.4%). In contrast, a gasoline-powered motorcycle has a range of around 180 miles (60 miles per gallon and a 3 gallon tank), while an electric motorcycle has a range of 100 to 170 miles. In this case, an electric motorcycle has about 55% to 95% of the gasoline-powered motorcycle range. Therefore, the electric car has just 20% of the gas-powered car range while the motorcycle enjoys 55-95%, demonstrating the relative advantage the electric motorcycles have in terms of driving distance between charges. One of the leading American electric motorcycle manufacturers, Zero Motorcycles, offers three electric motorcycle models with estimated range of 158 miles to 171 miles in city driving. Essentially, for electric motorcycles, range is not much of an issue.

Unfortunately, electric motorcycles must remain at premium prices. The market for electric motorcycles is not yet big enough for manufacturers to enjoy economies of scale. Electric motorcycles from Zero Motorcycles, however, can begin to compete with Harley Davidson, Victory, and Indian given that these motorcycles already command premium prices.

The Power of the Electric Vehicle:

When Americans think of electric vehicles, they don't think of the racetrack. They don't think of revving, big-engined vehicles. However, electric vehicles have a surprising, powerful performance. Big gasoline engines are sentimental: they powered our muscle cars in the 1960's. These muscle cars had impressive top speeds. However, in a world where driving at 100-150+ mph is impractical—if sentimental- people now focus on acceleration as the key barometer of automotive performance. Acceleration performance finds the electric cars winning the race against gasoline-powered cars. Torque drives acceleration. Torque is "a force that causes rotation." Internal combustion engines experience increasing torque as the engine's revolutions per minute (RPM) increase. In other words, as your car goes faster, your torque improves. An electric car or motorcycle, however, finds maximum torque almost immediately.

Road and Track Magazine did a review of the Tesla S Performance fully electric car model in February 2013. Technicians tested Tesla's claim that the car could accelerate from 0-60 mph in just 4.4 seconds. According to the magazine's reviews: "Tesla is wrong. Our car did it in 4.1 seconds."[115] Let's put this number in perspective. One of the best cars in the world: the 2014 Corvette Stingray boasts a 460 horsepower engine; it accelerates from 0-60 in 3.8 seconds. Tesla is a brand new American car manufacturer already competing with the best in the world, electric or not.

10

Electric Utilities:
More Changes on the Horizon

The past 20 years have brought massive change and competitive disruption to large American industries. One catalyst for these changes has, of course, been the Internet. However, deregulation, more efficient business models, and fresh communications technologies have pushed these changes as well. Amazon has out-competed many retailers, cell phones have reduced the landline business, Wal-Mart has eliminated the charming local mom and pop shops, and many airlines have been bankrupted or forced into mergers while competing with low-cost carriers. Even the U.S. postal service takes a hit from its competition with Federal Express and UPS. Innovation attacks historical business models. The question we must address is this: will the United States' electric utility companies face the same types of painful changes in the future?

The United States electrical grid is the largest machine in the world, connecting 3,200 utilities.[116] Electric utilities don't capture the country's imagination like Google, Facebook, or Apple. There hasn't been a movie like *The Social Network* revealing the romantic truth behind the electrical grid. However, the electric utilities are central players in the expanding shale and renewable power revolutions. The electric utility sector is the greatest energy-producer and claims the largest consumer-base in the United States. Therefore, it is important to analyze how innovation and changing business models will impact the sector. These regulated monopolies: the electric utilities affect everything. They sit

65

squarely at the intersection of technology, economics, politics, and energy policy. And the pressure to change and reshape their business models will continue to grow.

The Electric Utility's Business Model

Today's electric utility industry's business model consists of local, highly- regulated, centralized power generators connected to a highly-integrated electric grid. However, this business model has begun to erode. Already, distributed generation from solar and wind power is growing rapidly (admittedly from a small base). As more solar and wind power is utilized and other sources come online (geothermal, fuel cells, etc.), the United States will require less centralized power generation. Microgrids, for example, which power new real estate communities through local, clean energy resources, are already spreading across the country.

Incredibly, an inflection point will form when solar power costs fall to the same level as wholesale electric power prices. Afterwards, solar power use will grow exponentially. This inflection could form over the next 4-10 years. When solar reaches this competitive tipping point, a new source of distributed power will erupt. This switch in utility usage could mean a decrease in electric grid operations and centralization. Over the past twenty years, deregulation has established regional Independent System Operators in electricity markets, thus escalating this transition from a centralized electric grid controlled by utility companies to distributed power. Note: System Operators are independent organizations responsible for managing the day-to-day energy grid operations.

Distributed generation is escalating. Large companies like Google and Wal-Mart have recently contracted directly with wind and solar power developers to buy power under long term Power Purchase Agreements. The American Wind Energy Association (AWEA) recently reported that new wind power purchasers included at least 18 industrial buyers, 11 schools and universities, and eight towns or cities.[117]

Further purchasers of wind power include Anheuser-Busch, Nestle Corp, and Safeway.[118] According to AWEA, non-utility customers purchased 174 MW of wind power in 2012.[119]

Shale Revolution and its Effect on Electric Utilities and Business Models:

Major issues impacting electric utilities are climate change, volatile energy prices, regulation of returns on equity, state regulation, inconsistent deregulation, service outages, and demand side management. The greatest impact in recent years, however, has been the shale revolution; it has impacted many corners of electric utility companies' operations.

Between the 1930's and the 1960's, when electric utility companies became highly regulated, the business was relatively stable and predictable. However, the 1970's and early 1980's brought hard times: the utility sector found itself working through the United States' painful nuclear construction program. Furthermore, the 1970's oil shocks brought increased fuel costs for electric utilities and, in turn, higher costs for electric utility customers.

The late 1980's, however, brought Reagan Administration-sponsored deregulation to many heavily-regulated sectors like interstate natural gas pipelines, telephone service providers (breakup of the AT&T monopoly), and commercial airlines and trucking. (Note: the federal government regulates interstate commerce.) Deregulating these sectors was not painless; however, state politicians and regulators began to consider the potential benefits of deregulating the electric utility sector. The idea was this: power sector deregulation would allow electricity consumers to benefit from competition among electricity generators (companies that would generate electric power). They would compete for electric power sales to transmission and distribution companies (the operations involved in maintaining the transmission wires and distributing power to homes, businesses, universities, hospitals, etc.). This competition would lower prices for the average electricity consumer. This business structure was a fairly radical departure from the historical structure. The historical structures included vertically integrated utilities: they generated electricity from self-owned power plants and distributed electric power to customers.

By the mid-1990's, electric utility deregulation was in full swing. Many states required or allowed electric utilities to sell their electric power plant capacities to new or existing independent power producers. For example, Sithe Energies bought the generating capacity (power plants) of Boston Edison (now NSTAR) in mid-1996; a year or so later, they bought the generating assets (various power plants) from General Public Utilities in Pennsylvania, as well.

The Switch to Natural Gas in Top Electric Utility Companies:

Natural gas increased its electricity production from petroleum and coal over the past four decades. Petroleum and coal fell from 17.8% and 43.8% of electric power in 1973 to 0.6% and 41.4%, respectively, in 2012.[120] Natural gas use for the electricity production rose from 19.0% to 24.3% over the same period.[121] However, changes since 2005 highlight the dramatic shift towards the use of natural gas for fueling electric power generators. The following is a summary of the fuel sources for some of United States' leading electric utility companies and how they have increased natural gas usage over time:

Electric Utilities Using More Natural Gas: Table 10-1

2005 / 2013 (Generation Fuels)	Natural Gas (%)	Coal (%)	Nuclear (%)	Other (%)
American Electric Power	6.0 / 13.0	83.0 / 75.0	10.0 / 11.0	1.0 / 1.0
Duke Energy (1)	0.1 / 21.3	52.5 / 35.7	45.7 / 28.7	1.7 / 14.3
Public Service Enterprise Group	13.0 / 31.0	31.0 / 15.0	55.0 / 55.0	1.0 / 0.0
Southern Company	11.0 / 40.0	71.0 / 39.0	15.0 / 17.0	3.0 / 4.0

Source: Securities and Exchange Commission. Public company filings. (1) Merged with Progress Energy in July 2012.

The shale revolution and the "war" on coal have changed the generation profile of the United States' top electric utility companies. Natural gas captured coals' significant market share in the years since 2005.

Aside from low costs, the benefits of using natural gas from a utilities' perspective are the following:

- Lower greenhouse gas emissions than coal.
- Natural gas can be used as fuel for base load, intermediate and peaking generation capacity.
- Reliability.
- Dispatchability: ability to turn on gas turbines and ramp up output as needed.
- Provides backup generation for wind and solar.
- Relatively short construction timelines for gas compared to coal plants.

Electricity prices have fallen from 2008 to 2013. This is partially due to the Great Recession. However, much of this is due to lower natural gas prices from the shale gas boom. Let's analyze the precise reasons why. Generally, electric utility companies produce electricity from each power plant based on the marginal cost of fuel. Marginal cost of fuel is based on the costs associated with producing the next Mwh of electricity from coal, natural gas, wind, hydroelectric, or solar power. Some of these production costs are predetermined: those under long-term power purchase agreements associated with most wind or solar projects; others are variable: natural gas or coal prices are set according to a floating price index that changes with the commodity market.

Dispatch Curve or Merit Order:

How do electric utilities decide which power plants and fuels to use when managing their electricity production on an hour-to-hour basis? The system of meeting base load power needs with least expensive fuel and meeting peak power needs with the most expensive fuel is called the dispatch curve or merit order. Let's analyze how this all works.

Generally, electric utilities use the most economical fuels first (lowest marginal costs) to provide their base load capacity. Their base load capacity is the generation of electric power they need to meet a city, state, or region's basic electricity needs. Historically, coal-fired power plants provided this base load power; these days, however natural gas supplies a growing percentage of the base load power, as shown above in Table 10-1.

Beyond the base load power, there lies the intermediate load power. Things like increased electricity due to early morning school and business lights vary this intermediate demand. The next least expensive fuel meets this intermediate load power demand. This fuel is often natural gas.

Occasionally, unexpected events like heat waves cause electric power demand to spike. In this case, utilities must use the last and most expensive fuel supply available. This can be natural gas used by peaking plants, which are less-efficient power plants. They are generally less efficient because they must sit idle or at low production levels before ramping to meet the peak power demand. However, they do ramp up and down (produce more or less electric power) quite quickly and effectively.

Historical Electric Power Sources:

As aforementioned, coal was the cheapest source of electric power in the United States. There were several reasons for its usage. Historically, it provided the base load power generation capacity. It was the cheapest (due to economies of scale) when its power plants ran at or near full capacity. Unfortunately, technical reasons disallowed coal plants to scale production up and down very easily or economically.

Up until the recent shale boom, however, coal provided more than 50% of United States' generating capacity. Natural gas, however, was more expensive (with volatile prices); therefore, it provided the fuel for the intermediate load. Coal has lost its market share to natural gas. Gas prices have decreased due to growing supplies of shale gas.

United States' nuclear power plants generated nuclear power with historical consistency. Recently, however, nuclear power experienced a global growth decline. This decline is, in part, due to safety questions after the 2012 earthquake and tsunami at Japan's Fukushima nuclear power plant. Afterwards, global nuclear generation capacity increased by just 4.2 Gigawatts (GW), or 1.1%, to 373.1 GW in 2012.[122] Only 75 GW were added in 2012 versus the 296 GW added over the previous 25 years.[123]

Ironically, the United Arab Emirates provides a major exception to this decline. They are in the process of becoming the first country in the Arab world to have nuclear power. Recently, their $20 billion, 5,600 MW project was awarded to a South Korean construction contractor.[124] Despite its location at the center of the Arab world—the historic producer of oil and gas—the United Arab Emirates has committed enormous funds to become a leader in clean and renewable energy. Furthermore, Abu Dhabi Future Energy Company has invested in renewable energy projects domestically and around the world. The Company developed Masdar City, a new city designed and built around maximizing use of clean energy and sustainability.

Recent Nuclear Power in the United States:

Between about 2000 and 2007, the electric utility industry in the United States considered building new nuclear power plants for the first time in more than 20 years. Utility executives understood that coal was under increasing environmental, regulatory scrutiny. At the same time, concern about natural gas' rising costs (with expectations of required imports of liquefied natural gas) and the continuing volatility of gas prices struck a real chord. Furthermore, several utility industry leaders believed that nuclear plant technology had advanced enough that it warranted consideration as a source for new generating capacity additions. After the most recent 20 years of operating experience, the sector had proven its safety and operating strengths. Because new coal-fired power generation capacity was facing significant regulatory barriers, nuclear power became an alternative form of base-load capacity for electric utilities that could help replace coal over time.

The nuclear power construction cycle of the 1970's and 1980's, however, was very difficult for the electric utility sector. Nuclear power plant construction completions were delayed; cost overruns were in the range of billions of dollars. At that time, this technology was expected to result in very low electric power rates for utility customers. Unfortunately, it resulted in higher power costs and losses. These losses were sustained by shareholders and electric utility rate payers.

Recent extensive shale gas production resulted in lower natural gas prices across the United States. This has put downward pressure on electric power prices across the country. Since October 2012, electric power companies have announced the retirement of four nuclear reactors at three power plants. The four reactors have a combined capacity of nearly 3,600 MW.[125] The recent retirements are the first since 1998. The generating plants to close are the San Onofre Nuclear Generating Stations (2,150 MW), Kewaunee Power Station (556 MW), Crystal River Nuclear Plant (860 MW), and the Oyster Creek Nuclear Generating Station.[126]

Nuclear power plants have long lead times for permitting and construction. Therefore, several nuclear plants across the United States will be completed in the next few years, whether or not they are price competitive with natural gas. The competition between nuclear and natural-gas-fired turbines is not related to cost of fuel but rather the enormous capital costs for initial construction and ongoing maintenance. There are five new plants, for example under construction and ready for completion between 2001 and 2018. These plants will add 4,500 MW of generating capacity. [127]

Electric utilities face continued challenges as they deal with price uncertainly, spending billions on the electric grid, constructing new generation capacity, regulatory uncertainty, and raising and deploying large amounts of new capital. Fundamental business model changes and distributed generation and energy storage layer over these challenges, as well, and become great, future risk factors.

11

The Death of America's Coal Industry?

Coal: The Blissful Early Years

The story of coal mining is woven like fabric through the history of the United States. Much like the oil and gas industry, fortunes have been gained and lost by coal companies and developers. In the early years, after the civil war, coal replaced wood in its own energy revolution. This replacement of these energy resources extended through the Great Depression and World War II. These coal years brought both turmoil and comfort. Coal miners risked their own safety (methane explosions and collapsing mines) and long-term health (black lung disease) to support their families and fuel the United States' emergence as a global industrial super power. Civilians utilized coal to heat their homes; the military used it to power war ships; companies pushed it to make steel products; electric utilities used it to supply power for the growing middle class' necessities and luxuries. Today's coal will very likely not regain its former dominance in the energy industry; however, we should not overlook its huge contribution.

The War Against Coal:

The United States' recent shale revolution has had a profound impact on the coal industry. Until the past few years, the coal industry had provided the largest source of energy for electric power production. The United States was, essentially, the Saudi Arabia of coal for much of the 20th century. Coal, which someone once described as "flammable dirt," has been an economic boon due to its abundance, relatively low cost, and ability to provide base load electric power generating capacity.

The coal industry has provided relatively well-paying jobs to thousands of coal miners and workers in related sectors, like railroads, throughout the 20th century. And our coal supply still exists, should we choose to utilize it. The coal we now have could supply America with energy for another 100-200 years. However, the inherent problem in burning coal is 1) natural gas has become cheap due to the shale gas revolution; 2) coal is a relatively "dirty" energy source as it emits significant amounts of CO_2 and other pollutants when burned; 3) natural gas plants have more operational flexibility than coal plants.

At the end of 2012, there were 557 coal-fired power plants operating in the United States. This number is down 12.0%; that's 76 plants down from 2002's 633.[128] In 2012, the United States consumed 825.7 million tons of coal to produce electricity.[129] This number is down a sharp 21.7% from the 1,046.8 million tons of coal used to generate electricity as recently as 2007.[130]

Political Fire:

President Obama's Administration directly assaults the coal industry. It has used its unilateral, executive powers through the Environmental Protection Agency (EPA) to impose strict regulations on coal-fired power plant permits. Environmental concerns rather than economic concerns appear to drive this political strategy.

PJM, the operator of the world's largest wholesale electricity market, located in the Eastern United States, predicts that approximately 14,000 MW of coal-fired generation (out of an installed capacity of 78,600 MW of coal fired generation) could be retired by 2015 due to these new permitting rules.[131]

This projected 17.8% drop in coal-fired capacity would open further market opportunities for natural gas, wind, and solar power. Already, the advent of cheap natural gas and proposed new limits on carbon dioxide emissions brought coal plant commissions to a virtual standstill.

According to the Energy Information Administration, not one of the 136 American electric power plants that opened or expanded generating capacity in 2013 burned coal. Of the 127 similar plants set to open or expand in 2014, only two will be coal-fired.[132]

More than 90 percent of the United States' mined coal is used by the U.S. electrical power industry. Home and business space heating has long used natural gas and electricity. Since the year 2000, the growth of coal-fired power generation has declined. As of 2012, for example, coal accounted for just 37% of electricity production in the United States, down from 50% in 2005.[133]

The Anti-Coal Effect on a Personal Level:

These statistics seem to show the United States moving toward a more environmentally-conscious, more economically-feasible society. Wonderful. However, these statistics mask the unfortunate implications on historic coal states like West Virginia (Appalachia) and Wyoming (Powder River Basin). These coal-stocked areas are battered. Coal miners have very specific skills that do not transfer well to other industries. Employment in the coal mining industry declined 16.7% from 110,929 people in 1993 to 92,472 people in 2012.[134] Remember this: the lost coal-mining jobs are not executive management positions that pay $200,000 a year. These people are certainly not the wealthiest 1%. These jobs represent working-class people earning a hard $20,000 to $40,000 per year. However, the people retaining these jobs maintain the same American dream to send their children to college and have a decent retirement. How we help retrain and transition these displaced coal workers to other sectors is an important conversation that politicians should be having on a national basis.

A Closer Look at the Environmental Insight:

Environmentalists attacked the coal sector well before the onset of the shale revolution. Coal is a relatively dirty fuel: when it burns, it yields significant amounts of carbon dioxide, sulfur dioxide, nitrous oxides, and mercury.

Environmentalists are further outraged about coal mining. For example, it sometimes involves deforesting and scraping off entire mountain-tops—thus eliminating beautiful portions of our landscape. Further, coal opponents claim the negative health impacts on its workers. Black lung disease is not uncommon in coal miners, for example. Therefore, environmental groups sparked this coal battle; however, based on aforementioned facts, the shale gas revolution effectively ended it.

Environmentalists, Politicians, and the Power Plant:

Environmental organizations have focused on reducing power plant coal burning. They assisted in electing President Barack Obama who, during his first presidential campaign, promised to bankrupt any company choosing to build new coal-fired power plants. Note: ironically, the oil and gas industry's competition reduced coal consumption the most over the past 5-10 years.

These days, new coal-fired power plants have a difficult time obtaining their appropriate permits. On June 26th, 2013, President Obama gave a speech on global warming and announced that he would direct the U.S. EPA to initiate new restrictions on relicensing existing coal plants as well. The President appears to have strengthened his anti-coal agenda and he is well known for relying on his executive powers rather than fighting with a stale-mated Congress.

MATS and the Clean Up:

The new Mercury and Air Toxics (MATs) regulations will require the electric utility industry to spend millions cleaning up existing coal plants. On March 28, 2013, the EPA finalized their emission limits for new power plants under the Mercury and Air Toxics Standards.[135] This includes emission limits for mercury, particulate matter (PM), sulfur dioxide (SO_2), acid gases, and certain individual metals.[136] Additionally, certain monitoring and testing requirements will be adjusted for new sources. The new standards affect only future-built coal and oil-fired power plants. The update does not change the final emission limits or other requirements for existing power plants.

The Obama Administration Raises the Stakes:

On June 2nd, 2014, the Obama Administration, through the Environmental Protection Agency, escalated its attacks on carbon emissions.[137] They released their proposed "Clean Power Plan". The plan calls for a 30% reduction in carbon emissions by each state's power plants from 2005 levels by the year 2030.[138] The individual states may choose how to implement the Clean Power Plan. However, if they choose to defy the federal government and not adopt a plan, the EPA will impose one on any state not in compliance.

In general, this initiative sounds like it is based on laudable goals, depending on your view of the threat posed by climate change. However, as is always the case, the devil is in the details. The Clean Power Plan requires each state by June 30, 2016 to come up with plans to lower carbon emissions by their fleet of power plants.[139] Each state will have a goal to reach, the level (in percentage terms) of which will be determined by the following formula: CO_2 emissions from fossil-fuel fired plants in pounds (lbs) divided by state electricity generation from fossil-fuel fired power plants and certain low -or zero- emitting power sources in megawatt hours.[140]

Gina McCarthy, the EPA Administrator, framed the issue as a way to reduce asthma in children across the United States, a pathway to lower medical costs, and a means to reduce the enormous financial impacts of natural disasters, like Hurricane Sandy, which some people believe are occurring more frequently due to climate change.[141] A central benefit of the proposed Clean Power Plan, according to the EPA, is that each state is given a great deal of flexibility in designing and implementing their plans. Each state has the flexibility to reach the percentage rate target by encouraging more efficient use of fossil plants, switching from high carbon fuels to low carbon ones (like coal to natural gas) or using more renewable energy of any type.

Who will be hurt most if this plan is fully implemented? Coal producers. The easiest way for states to comply is for their local electric utilities to reduce the use of coal and increase natural gas. Existing nuclear power plants may also see their utilization increased as they are zero-carbon sources of electricity. Consumers are unlikely to see any major impact on their bills as a result of program as natural gas plants do not run at full capacity and therefore existing plants can be better utilized once coal capacity is further reduced.

A Note on Environmental Groups:

Environmental groups are necessary to keep potential polluters in line. However, they are businesses. Environmental organizations raise money, pay salaries, buy services, pay for consultants and, in some cases, reward their leaders with attractive compensation packages. They also employ well-paid lobbyists to advance their agenda with legislatures at both the state and federal levels. There is nothing wrong with this. It is just worth keeping these facts in mind while debating the merits of any number of environmental issues.

We must analyze both environmental attacks on hydraulic fracturing and coal sectors. This is because the environmentalists have essentially "done their duty" with the coal sector. They've succeeded. Now, however, the environmentalist's agenda appears to target the shale oil and gas revolution. They are attempting to stop or slow down any fossil fuel forward progress. They want to leave the United States with "carbon-free" renewable energy as the only "viable" source for energy supplies. There is nothing inherently wrong with this agenda. However, consumers, voters, business executives, and politicians must remain aware of the agenda's numerous implications with regards to cost advantage of shale energy versus renewable energy.

Coal Comes Back Around?

Technological advances could change the "balance of power" back towards coal. The industry has talked extensively about clean coal. However, the technology has not advanced fast enough or the technology remains uneconomical. For example, a few years ago brought a heightened interest in gasifying coal and using this cleaner gas to burn in electric power plants.

Coal to liquid processes were considered as well; many of these technologies lost funding after the 2009 economic recession.

Coal VS. Natural Gas Threat:

How has the coal industry responded to the market share threat posed by natural gas in recent years? Their strategy now focuses on exports. U.S. coal is exported to every region in the world. The Energy Information Administration projected a third straight year of more than 100 million short tons of coal exports in 2013. This follows annual 2011 exports of 107.3 million short tons and record annual 2012 exports of 107.3 million. United States to Asia coal exports have increased from 2% in 2007 to 25% in 2012. The four largest export markets for American coal in 2012 were China, Japan, India, and South Korea. The top five destinations for exported coal in March 2013 (in descending order) were China, The Netherlands (a large transshipment point), the United Kingdom, South Korea and Brazil.

Top 10 Coal Producers in the United States: Table 11-1

Rank	Company	Production (short tons)	Percent of Total Production
1	Peabody Energy	202,237,000	25.5
2	Arch Coal Inc.	160,279,000	20.2
3	Alpha Natural Resources LLC	116,394,000	14.7
4	Cloud Peak Energy	95,596,000	12.0
5	CONSOL Energy Inc.	62,089,000	7.8
6	Cerrejon Coal Company	33,300,000	4.2
7	Alliance Resource Operating Partners LP	32,949,000	4.2
8	Energy Future Holdings Corp.	32,610,000	4.1
9	Peter Kiewit Sons Inc.	29,998,000	3.8
10	NACCO Industries Inc.	27,904,000	3.5
	Total	**793,356,000**	**100.0%**

Data is for 2011. Source Energy Information Administration, http://www.eia.gov/coal/annual/pdf/table10.pdf

Export Strategy Revels in Continued Greenhouse Gas Emissions:

A pure business and profit maximization standpoint says the coal industry's export strategy is logical and effective. The critical problem, however, lies with the global environment. The exported coal is burned in another country, resulting in the same greenhouse gas emissions. There is only one global environment. Global warning stares us all, global citizens, in the face.

The American coal industry's export strategy, however, faces decreasing demand from international markets as well. China, a key export market for American coal, recently reduced its demand for imported coal. China's economic growth is slowing, and they are fighting critical air pollution levels, particularly in Beijing, Shanghai, and Guangzhou. Therefore, China is increasing its already aggressive renewable energy generation growth. This decreased demand is causing the American coal price advantage to slip. United States' 2013 coal exports declined about 3.5% to 110 million tons from 2012's record exports of 114 million metric tons.[142]

Does all of this doom and gloom mean that the final nails have been placed in the U.S. coal industry's coffin? Not necessarily. Yes, the shale energy revolution has had its greatest impact on the coal sector in the United States. However, coal is still enormously important fuel source around the world. Also, as the U.S. begins to export natural gas as LNG starting in 2016, and more truck fleets use natural gas, gas prices could start trending up once again. A particularly important wild card for the coal industry is the Presidential election of 2016. Coal sector supporters argue that having a new, conservative administration in the White House would improve the condition of the coal sector.

Finally, there is the wild card that is always present in every corner of the energy sector: innovation. The term clean coal may seem like an oxymoron. However, the coal industry and others have worked for decades to improve technology of devices, called scrubbers, which clean the power plant exhaust gases and smoke before they enter the atmosphere. Scrubbers can remove sulfur, nitrogen oxide and CO_2. The challenge is that these technologies are quite expensive. Owners of coal-fired power plants spent $30 billion on flue gas desulfurization systems (scrubbers) from 2007 to 2011.[143] Given the strong regulatory and economic incentives for electric utilities to move away from coal, scrubber manufactures will need to aggressively innovate in the years ahead to lower costs.

12

Master Limited Partnerships - Financing the Revolution

So, how did America finance the hundreds of billions of dollars of infrastructure and drilling operations needed to develop these massive shale resources? They did it with bank loans, bonds and equity (private and public). However, Master Limited Partnerships (MLPs) played a key role. MLP's meet the enormous capital needs of the U.S. oil and gas sector; they are well-positioned to benefit from the shale energy revolution growth. The past 15 years' oil and gas industry's use of MLPs has yielded effective capital attraction.

Lack of Double Taxation:

An MLP is a form of legal structure, like a hybrid of a partnership and a corporation. With this hybrid, it maintains one important benefit: MLPs avoid double taxation of earnings at the corporate and investor levels. For example, let's say that Behemoth Brothers Oil and Gas Corporation has $100 of earnings before taxes. They pay 35% in taxes and pay the remaining $65 out to their investors as dividends. That dividend is considered income to the investor. The investor must pay tax on that income as well; for example, he'll pay 15% or $9.75. Now, the result is that the $100 of pre-tax corporate earnings is now $55.25 of investor after-tax income. The income has effectively been taxed twice.

MLPs' income is paid directly to investors without corporate taxes. The income is taxed at the investor level only. In our example, then,

$100 is paid to investors as distributions (not referred to as dividends), and $24 is paid in taxes, thereby leaving $76 dollars as after-tax income. This looks much better than the $55.25 after-tax income in the double taxation traditional corporation scenario. (Note: this is a very simplified example.)

Sure, MLPs' structure lacks all the glamour of a new Hollywood movie—or whatever new "App" people are into these days. However, the existence of MLPs is incredibly exciting from the shale energy revolution standpoint. MLP's have raised billions of debt and equity capital for the oil and gas industry. A recent bill was introduced in Congress that would permit the inclusion of certain renewable energy assets into existing or new MLPs. This would allow large sources of equity for renewable energy asset development and acquisition. This is discussed in more detail in Chapter 24.

The table below summarizes some of the key differences between MLP's and Corporations.

MLP's Versus Corporations:Table 12-1

Feature	Master Limited Partnerships	Corporations
Security Type	Units	Shares
Taxation Level	Unitholder	Corporate & Shareholder
Tax forms for investors:	K-1's	1099's
Cash Payments referred to as:	Distributions	Dividends
Tax Treatment	50%-100% tax deferred	15%
Investor Base	Retail	Institutional
General Partner	Yes	No

Source: Merrill Lynch, Equity Research, May 9, 2013.

The MLP technicalities require that ideal assets in their MLP structure are those that generate stable cash flows. For example, natural gas pipelines generate very stable earnings and cash flows; therefore, natural gas and liquids pipeline assets are often in MLPs. Operations related to pipelines, such as the removal of natural gas liquids (ethane, butane, pentane, etc.) from wet natural gas (known as fractionation), are often important operating assets in midstream MLPs, as well.

MLP structure popularity has driven significant growth across the oil and gas sector in recent years. Since 2000, the number of energy MLPs has grown from 23 to 90.[144] 2012 was a record year for MLP equity raising with $22 billion raised, versus $16 billion in 2011.[145]

The past 6 years' explosion of Bakken formation oil production has forced a critical shortage of oil and gas gathering lines (networks of small diameter pipelines connecting oil wells to larger, often interstate liquids pipelines). Without this key infrastructure, oil producers in the Bakken have had to rely on railroads and trucks to ship the crude oil production to various refinery markets around the country. MLPs do not want to be left out of the Bakken production bonanza; therefore, they've begun their railway infrastructure investments. For example, December 2012 brought Plains All American Pipeline's acquisition of four crude oil rail terminals for $500 million.[146]

The MLPs investment in railway infrastructure is not without significant benefits. These benefits include shorter contract periods, lower upfront costs, and added shipping flexibility to a range of markets across the United States. The drawbacks to these investments occur when compared to the pipeline investments. Railway infrastructure includes higher transportation costs, higher barriers to entry, and relatively small investments in the context of overall capital expenditure programs.[147]

Kinder Morgan, Inc.

Richard Kinder, a former Vice Chairman of Enron, has been a leader and pioneer in the MLP area for many years. Mr. Kinder left Enron in 1996 after serving 16 years with the company.[148] He left Enron after apparently losing the CEO role to Jeff Skilling. Kinder is the founder of Kinder Morgan, a very large and successful MLP. Kinder Morgan. Inc. (KMI) has grown from a start-up to a very large organization—one that acquired El Paso Natural Gas in 2011. KMI is now the owner and operator of two large MLPs: Kinder Morgan Energy Partners and El Paso Pipeline Partners. With the inclusion of these acquisitions, KMI owns or operates approximately 80,000 miles of pipelines and 180 refined products terminals.[149] Their pipelines transport natural gas, refined petroleum products, crude oil, and carbon dioxide (CO_2), and other products. Richard Kinder accepts a salary of $1 per year. You read that correctly: $1 per year. He enhances his reputation as an authenticate leader. Kinder's doing just fine on his $1 yearly salary. He's a self-made energy leader with an estimated net worth of $10.2 billion.[150]

Kinder Morgan has, in a way, become a "victim" of its own great success through the use of the MLP structure. Because the MLP structure requires payout of about 90% of annual cash flow to investors, there comes a point where a very large MLP, like Kinder Morgan, will want to grow internally and make more acquisitions rather than paying out a large portion of its cash flow. Having grown from a start-up to an energy behemoth (in the best possible sense of the word), the organization has decided to abandon the MLP structure and merge all of its energy operations into conventional corporations. On August 10, 2014, Kinder Morgan, Inc. announced that it was acquiring all of the equity interests in Kinder Morgan Energy Partners, Kinder Morgan Management and El Paso Pipeline Partners for combined consideration of about $71 billion.[151].

Does this transaction mean that the MLP structure is no longer attractive or is waning in popularity? Just the opposite is true. Both investors and energy companies are as eager as ever to place mid-stream (pipeline) and other fee-based assets into MLP's.

13

Revitalizing America's Liquefied Natural Gas Sector

The United States' liquefied natural gas sector has brought dependable natural gas imports for about 40 years. LNG is formed when the temperature of natural gas (methane or CH4) is lowered to -260 Fahrenheit and thereby converted from gas into liquid. Why would we want this? Essentially, liquid natural gas takes up 1/600th of the volume of gaseous natural gas. Therefore, the transportation is economically feasible. It is then, of course, turned back to gaseous form. Natural gas exports come from areas around the world with excess supplies like Qatar, Algeria, and Trinidad and Tobago. The LNG is transported on very large ships with giant cryogenic tanks. The United States is actually becoming a country with excess natural gas and is on its way to becoming a powerhouse in the global LNG markets. In the long run, this fact could benefit renewable energy producers. Our powerhouse status in LNG markets could very well raise natural gas prices and make renewable energy sources more price competitive.

Let's look at an actual American re-gasification plant. Boston's Everett Marine Terminal has imported more than 1,000 LNG shipments since 1971.[152] The once-rundown neighborhood's terminal provides natural gas to the Boston area and the 1,700 MW Mystic Power Plant located in Charlestown, Massachusetts. Much of the imported natural gas running through the Everett Terminal originated from Trinidad and Tobago and North Africa's Algeria. The historical benefit of delivering natural gas to downtown Boston was avoided bottlenecks among interstate pipelines, particularly during spells of brutally cold Boston weather.

A Quick Turnaround:

In 2004 and 2005, the American LNG sector focused solely on building re-gasification plants for importing natural gas from other countries. The ongoing decline of conventional natural gas reserves prior to 2005, rising drilling costs, and growing energy demand in the U.S. encouraged the building of LNG re-gasification plants on the East, West, and Gulf coasts of the United States.

By mid-2013, however, the view had shifted 180 degrees. The shale natural gas revolution had begun, creating an abundance of new natural gas supplies, LNG project developers, including Cheniere, began seeking United States Department of Energy approval to export natural gas as LNG to Europe and Asia.

This shocking switch is best recognized from a numerical point of view. Between 2000 and 2010, new investments worked toward natural gas importation and storage infrastructure; this was, of course, prompted by natural gas' low supply expectations and higher, volatile domestic prices. In the years after 2000, North America's LNG import capacity expanded from approximately 2.3 billion cubic feet per day to 22.7 BCFD, around 35% of the United States' average daily requirement. However, by 2012, U.S. consumption of imported LNG had fallen to less than .5 BCFD, leaving most of this capacity unused.[153] The EIA projects that the United States will become a net exporter of LNG in 2016, a net pipeline exporter in 2025, and a net exporter overall in 2021.[154]

Gloucester's Under Water Re-Gasification Plants:

Let's look at a dramatic example of this 180-degree turn. The example lies lifeless on the ocean floor about 30 miles offshore Gloucester, Massachusetts. Gloucester, a beautiful fishing town with a rich 350-year history of sea ship captains, is an unlikely place for an LNG terminal. However, in the early 2000's, two companies decided to construct two deep-water LNG ports for a combined cost of $700-$750 million.[155] These projects were innovative ideas at the time; they would enable giant LNG tankers to offload their LNG cargoes from the sea rather than at a large re-gasification plant onshore. Gloucester, a beautiful, affluent, residential area of New England, would very likely not approve a new onshore LNG plant. The offshore technology allowed for the re-gasification of LNG right on the ships and the injection of the natural gas directly into an existing offshore natural gas pipeline. Now, less than a decade after deep-water construction began, the pipes, buoys, and risers lay unused at the bottom of the ocean. The shale revolution has made them useless. This is just one more example of how a consensus about America's energy future, requiring massive new natural gas imports, ultimately turned out to be wrong.

Cheniere:

At one time, the LNG business certainly did not evoke feelings of intense excitement. Fortunately, however, entrepreneur and energy innovator Charif Souki started a company called Cheniere Energy in the 1990's—changing the LNG business dramatically. He built Cheniere into the leading independent shareholder-owned LNG company in the United States. The purpose of Cheniere's formation was to build a number of new LNG re-gasification plants across the U.S. He and his team of entrepreneurs and innovators were capitalizing on 1990's and 2000's expectation that the United States import an increasing amount of natural gas at competitive prices. Of course, being at the forefront of LNG re-gasification plant development enabled the company to see and quickly act on the rapid changes in the LNG markets since the occurrence of the shale gas revolution. They are now a leading developer of LNG export terminals.

Outline of United States LNG Terminal Infrastructure: Table 13-1

LNG Terminals	Location	Owner	Size	Completed or Expected Completion
Kenai LNG	Nikiski, Alaska	ConocoPhillips	NA	1969
Dominion Cove Point	Lusby, Maryland	Dominion	1.8 BCFD	1978 (first shipments)
Southern LNG	Elba Island, Georgia	Southern LNG (El Paso Corp. / KMI)	1.2 BCFD	1978
Trunkline LNG	Lake Charles, Louisiana	Southern Union / Energy Transfer	2.0 BCFD(1)	2018(2)
EcoElectrica	Punta, Guyanilla, Puerto Rico	Gas Natural, International Power & Mitsui	NA	NA
Golden Pass LNG	Jefferson County, Texas	Qatar Petroleum, ExxonMobil and ConocoPhillips (3)	2.0 BCFD	2011
Sabine Pass LNG	Cameron Parish, Louisiana	Cheniere Energy / Cheniere Energy Partners	4.0 BCFD	2008
Cameron LNG	Cameron Parish, Louisiana	Sempra LNG	1.5 BCFD	2009
Freeport LNG	Freeport, Texas	ConocoPhillips and Michael Smith(4)	2.0 BCFD	2008
Everett Marine Terminal	Everett, Massachusetts	GDF Suez, Distrigas	1.0 BCFD	1971
Gulf LNG	Pascagoula, Mississippi	Kinder Morgan, GE & others(5)	1.3 BCFD	2011

Source: alaska.conocophillips.com, www.dom.com, www.hydro-carbons-technology.com, www.goldenpasslng.com, www.cheniere.com, www.cameron.sempralng.com, www.FreeportLNG.com, www.suezenergyna.com, www.kindermorgan.com Note: the list above does not include 3 deep-water ports located in the Gulf of Mexico and offshore Gloucester, Massachusetts. 1) Proposed size after completion of 3 "trains" (modular units). 2) Proposed initial operating date for new export capacity. 3) Qatar Petroleum, ExxonMobil and ConocoPhillips ownership stakes in Golden Pass LNG are 70%, 17.6% and 12.4%, respectively. 4) There are also Limited Partners, including Zachry, Dow, and Osaka Gas. 5) Kinder Morgan (50%), General Electric (46%), and other investors (4.0%).

LNG Liquefaction Plants by the Numbers:

2 billion cubic feet per day of natural gas: does this mean anything to you? Let's try to put this number into perspective. Okay? The cube root of 2 billion cubic feet is 1,259.92 feet. Therefore, a cube with a length, width, and height of 1,259.92 feet has a volume of 2 billion cubic feet. Imagine a line extending 4.2 football fields in front of you and another extending 4.2 football fields beside you (at a 90 degree angle), and a vertical line extending up from you for 1,259.92 feet. The height would be almost as high as the original World Trade Center towers at 1,362 and 1,368 feet. This area you visualize in front of you, beside you, and above you equals 2 billion cubic feet. This area is the amount of natural gas that many of these LNG liquefaction plants can process each day.

Domestic Natural Gas vs. Global Natural Gas Markets:

As we've discussed, the United States is evolving its purely domestic natural gas market to one ready to dominate the global natural gas market. The natural gas market 40 years ago, however, was largely a regional U.S. domestic market. New interstate gas pipelines, the trading of futures contracts, new over-the-counter trading platforms (Enron Online, Intercontinental Exchange), standardized bilateral supply contracts, and deregulation (starting in the 1980's) transformed this regional market makeup into a national market. Now, we're heading toward a truly global natural gas market based on LNG. In recent years, Qatar, Trinidad and Tobago, and Australia have dominated LNG exports to energy-constrained countries like China, Japan, and South Korea. LNG demand has skyrocketed over the past ten years as Europe seeks to diversify its supplies from Russian gas imports. Most recently,

Japan sought increased supplies after the Fukushima nuclear plant accident in 2012.

European natural gas prices are significantly higher than United States prices. Historically, natural gas prices in Europe have been indexed to the price of crude oil. Oil price increases over the past 6 years have forced European natural gas prices to the roof. For example, the average price for natural gas in the UK, Germany, and Japan (imported as LNG) were $9.46, $11.03 and $16.75 per mm BTU's in 2012.[156]

Compare these insane prices to United States' natural gas average price of $2.75 - $5.50 per mm BTU (Henry Hub price). The price arbitrage between the U.S. and Europe/Asia provides enormous opportunity for the United States to export natural gas quite profitably. Over time these price differentials may narrow; in the short and intermediate term, billions in export earnings await.[157]

The rise of Russian nationalism under Vladimir Putin and the annexation of Crimea in mid-2014 has raised the energy security stakes for Europe even further. Europe will be a strong market for American LNG and possibly for crude oil exports, if the U.S. government ultimately decides to lift the ban on crude oil exports.

The Panama Canal:

Panama Canal expansion, of all things, may become a very important catalyst for boosting United States' LNG market dominance. The Panama Canal began a $5.25 billion expansion to capture Asian-made consumer and industrial products shipments to the U.S. East Coast; however, the flow of liquefied natural gas in the opposite direction promises to be a better bet.[158] For example, Texas—the Panama Canal neighbor and an obvious leader in oil and gas—could increase exports of natural gas produced from its Barnett Shale. A surge in U.S. natural gas production means that new shale and conventional gas projects in Australia, East Africa, Canada, and Russia cannot export LNG to the United States; they must focus more on Asian sales.[159] With the price of American natural gas quite low and our gas resources close to the Panama Canal, however, the United

States will have a strong competitive advantage relative to LNG exporters around the world.

Becoming a major LNG global exporter essentially realizes the American dream. We are self-sufficient and able to compete globally. Thanks to the shale energy revolution, it is hard to imagine a better scenario.

14

Opening New Natural Gas Markets

The Transportation Sector:

The United States has the historic opportunity to increase the natural gas used in the transportation sector. Natural gas is cleaner than oil (fewer greenhouse gas emissions), and we still rely on imported crude oil from OPEC right now. Of course, the future will be a different story. Domestic natural gas could play an important role in decreasing our addiction to foreign oil. The United States oil is used primarily for transportation—and this fact hasn't changed in quite some time. In 1973, petroleum provided 95.8% of all the transportation sector energy while natural gas provided only 4.0%. 39 years later, in 2012, petroleum continues to provide 92.5% of the transportation energy; natural gas provided just 2.9%.[160] Note: both petroleum and natural gas lost market share over this period. This is because renewable fuels (ethanol, biodiesel, etc) rose from providing 0.0% in 1973 to 4.3% in 2012. Natural gas has a clear opportunity to grow its market share vis-a-vis petroleum.[161]

Energy leaders, most notably T. Boone Pickens, the self-made energy billionaire, have argued for years that the United States should use more compressed natural gas (CNG) to power its trucks. CNG has been technologically ready for decades, and many truck-operation companies and bus-operation municipalities have already adopted CNG. CNG works well for local, round-trip type applications like parcel delivery. Trucks can go back to a depot at night for refueling by the next morning.

There are, of course, some drawbacks to CNG. CNG has a lower energy density; therefore, the CNG-fueled trucks' range is less than LNG-fueled trucks' range. Also, due to required compression, refueling of CNG powered trucks can take longer. Wide-spread adoption of CNG, however, would further reduce American reliance on imported oil over the next 10-20 years.

Companies are improving technologies that will enable truck fleet operators to power more of their trucks with LNG. In 2010, only 40 public and private LNG refueling sites existed to serve 3,354 LNG vehicles.[162] However, these numbers are likely to grow over time. The technology of storage tanks and insulation will improve, and fleet operators will realize the benefits of natural gas versus diesel fuel. LNG powered trucks are generally used for long haul routes as the higher energy density of LNG vs. CNG affords greater driving ranges between stops. Here are the numbers: LNG contains 2.4 times more energy per diesel gallon than CNG.[163] Furthermore, LNG is a liquid. Refueling an LNG truck is quicker and easier than refueling a CNG truck.

Creating CNG-powered vehicles brings the next logical step in increasing natural gas utilization. Cost, safety, or performance considerations, however, result in low general public demand for compressed natural gas cars. This shows the classic "chicken or egg" dilemma: large numbers of people won't buy compressed natural gas cars because there are not enough filling stations. Conversely, companies won't build thousands of new filling stations because there are not enough CNG cars on the road.

The Cost of Conversion:

Some of the challenges associated with conversion of a significant percentage of our automobiles from gasoline to compressed natural gas include the following:

- The cost to retrofit 157,000 gas stations.
- Compressors in our homes will cost money, require changes in building codes, and likely require the industry to obtain Public Utilities Commission approval.

- Natural gas prices have historically been volatile due to weather, pipeline bottlenecks, etc.
- The cost of retrofitting cars to burn CNG rather than gasoline.
- Industrial users of natural gas, like chemicals manufacturers, don't want to compete with another source of natural gas demand.

Below is an outline of the costs of converting only a small portion of American automobiles to compressed natural gas:

- 232 million cars, pickups, and SUV's registered in the U.S.[164]
- Estimate of CNG conversion costs of $9,250/car (average of $6,500-$12,000 estimated range).[165]
- Assumed goal for conversion: 5% per year for 5 years (conversion of old cars, not new sales). Total conversions: 25% of cars on the road.

Total estimated cost: $107.3 billion per year or $536.5 billion over 5 years. The second major cost lies in the required capital to convert gas stations to ones offering CNG.

- Conversion of 157,000 gas stations at only $150,000 each equals $23.5 billion.
- Installation of gas compressors in 20 million homes at $2,000 per home is $40 billion.

After all of these expenditures, 75% of cars in the United States would still run on gasoline. Clearly, there is a lot more work that must be done to bring down the cost of converting passenger cars to CNG and further developing the required infrastructure.

Fuel Cells:

Another gasoline alternative is the use of fuel cells to power electric cars. Fuel cells create electricity through a chemical process rather than a mechanical process. Fuel cell technology has been around for 20-30 years and it is rather scalable. For example, companies like

Bloom Energy use the fuel technology to power large buildings, while other fuel cell companies work on a wide range of new applications. Fuel cells require hydrogen. And where does this hydrogen come from? No surprise, here. The most abundant source of feasibly delivered hydrogen is natural gas. Fuel cell technology is growing in the United States. Hyundai planned to build 1,000 fuel cell vehicles for distribution in 2013, while Toyota suggested that production costs are decreasing quickly enough that fuel cell vehicle prices should fall to $50,000 by 2015.[166]

15

America: The World's Oil Refiner

The United States is a world leader in the production and export of refined oil products like gasoline, diesel, and jet fuel. The U.S. crude oil market is showing a key trend of rapid light, sweet crude oil growth for the refining sector. This trend is particularly strong in the middle third of the United States. The shale oil supplies from the Bakken formation in North Dakota have grown so quickly that truck and rail shipments are reaching capacity limits. No major liquid pipelines directly serve that area of the country. The refineries in the upper Midwest are blessed with ample crude oil while the infrastructure is lacking to transport this oil to key refineries located on the East and West Coasts of the United States. Because the Midwest lacks the refinery capacity to absorb all of these new shale oil supplies, the refineries on the Gulf Coast are the closest large markets for the Bakken shale oil. Billions of dollars, however, were invested in new crude oil pipeline capacity in order to bring the Bakken crude to United States' refinery hub.

United States oil refineries had total throughput capacity of 15.0 million barrels per day at the end of 2012 which was up 2.4% from 2008.[167] Currently, 65-70 refineries in the United States have potential access to shale oil supplies.[168] The United States train transportation sector capitalized on these pipeline constraints, offering Bakken area oil producers increased crude oil transportation capacity. North Dakota's rail export capacity stood at only 30,000 barrels per day in 2008; capacity grew to 965,000 barrels by the end of 2013.[169]

One way that oil refiners' benefit from the shale revolution is the lower prices for natural gas. Refineries are energy intensive; therefore, declining natural gas costs improve the profitability of refineries. We must understand the refinery sector's economics: under current U.S. law, crude oil may not be exported. However, refined products can and are exported to markets across the world.

Historically, the United States petroleum sector has faced refinery capacity constraints. For example, a new refinery hasn't been built in the United States since 1977.[170] During the 1980's and early 1990's, numerous small and older refineries closed due to chronic losses. In the 1990's, some integrated oil companies and independent refiners saw that the world's sources of crude oil decreased while prices for light, sweet crude increased. Therefore, they began sourcing supplies of heavy, sour crude from Venezuela and other countries.

More than half of all oil is used to make gasoline. Oil consumption fell from 19.68 million bpd in 2002 to 18.95 million bpd in 2012, a 3.7% decline over this 10-year period.[171] Fortunately, the United States has reduced its gasoline consumption.

16

Pipelines: Energy's Economic Arteries

We don't see our arteries, but we know they're there: pumping our blood to our heart and our brain. We couldn't survive without them, much like the American economy could not thrive without our energy pipelines. Natural gas and oil pipelines are the unseen, critically important infrastructure for the energy industry. We have a constant demand for natural gas, gasoline, and electricity. The oil and gas industry has spent decades designing, financing, building, and maintaining this colossal pipeline network to meet this need. This infrastructure is a huge national asset, an important component of American wealth. Therefore, the renewable energy industry must offer very compelling energy economics to justify the abandonment or reduction of these valuable assets. We've worked hard for these arteries: should we throw them away?

Many of the United States' natural gas pipelines were developed and built over the past 50-100 years. They were designed to transport natural gas and refined products from Texas, Louisiana, and Oklahoma to the Northeast, upper Midwest, and the west Coast. Other pipelines brought natural gas from Canada to New England, the upper Midwest, and Northern California. That's a lot of ground to cover.

Pipelines are operationally and economically efficient ways of transporting natural gas from production areas to local markets (homes, businesses, hospitals, nursing homes, etc.) across the United States. Pipelines reduce the number of trucks on the road and the associated truck emissions. This means reduced traffic and greenhouse gas emissions. The oil and gas industry operates about 305,000 miles of interstate and intrastate gas pipelines across the United States.[172] There are also tens of thousands of miles of crude and refined products pipelines.

Shale Revolution and Pipelines:

The birth and exponential growth of the shale gas revolution changed some of the transportation dynamics of the Northeast natural gas market. Now, because of the Marcellus shale, natural gas pipelines are built to bring Marcellus shale gas to regional markets. These new pipelines may reduce demand for transportation capacity on existing pipelines from the Gulf Coast region.

Factors including increased shale oil and gas supplies, lower prices, and increased demand have created a need for significant natural gas pipeline expansion. Changes in supply and demand require that an estimated 28,000 to 61,900 miles of new pipelines must be added in North America by 2030; this will require $108 to $163 billion worth of investment.[173] Additional natural gas storage capacity of 371 to 598 billion cubic feet will be required, as well, at a cost of $2 billion to $5 billion.[174]

The Marcellus shale's natural gas is very rich in natural gas liquids, like ethane. This is fortunate for the Pennsylvania, West Virginia and Ohio areas. New pipelines are proposed to transport ethane to the Gulf Coast, where most of the nation's plastics manufacturing plants reside. Enterprise Products Partners and Chesapeake Energy Corp., for example, announced plans to build a 1,230-mile (1,980 km) pipeline with 125,000-barrels/day capacity from the Marcellus and Utica production areas to the U.S. Gulf Coast. Note: this new pipeline would eventually connect to current pipelines. Because numerous domestic and international chemical companies have announced plans to build Gulf Coast-region manufacturing plants in the next 3-5 years, this new pipelines is of critical importance.

Keystone XL Pipeline:

The proposed environmentally-controversial Keystone XL Pipeline is a 1,179-mile (1,897 km), 36-inch diameter crude oil pipeline. With a projected cost of $5.3 billion, the pipeline could bring up to 9,000 direct American jobs across the upper Midwest.[175] The proposed pipeline will transport crude oil from the heavy oil sands production areas of Hardisty, Alberta to Nebraskan-origin pipelines that extend to Cushing, Oklahoma. Gulf Coast oil refineries can then retrieve these new oil supplies (via the Cushing pipelines) from both the Canadian tar sands and the Bakken shale formation in North Dakota.[176]

Given that Canada is a strong ally to the United States and a stable democracy with close geographic proximity, it is in the United States' interest to import crude oil from Canada rather than Middle Eastern suppliers. We've certainly sent Saudi Arabia more than enough money; Venezuela is no ally; and Iraq's political vulnerability creates no real comfort. Furthermore, environmentalists' argument that billions in Middle East spending has been utilized to "keep the peace" certainly holds layers of truth. Therefore, approval of the Keystone XL Project would enhance energy security and provide thousands of construction jobs. Environmental issues and controversy aside, the Keystone pipeline would further lessen United States' reliance on Mideast oil. Perhaps it would eventually lessen our need for large military commitment to the area.

Environmentalists vs. Keystone Pipeline

Environmentalists hold strong opposition to the Xl Keystone Pipeline. Their strong opposition caused the Obama Administration to strategically postpone the pipeline approval until after the presidential election in 2012. This has been covered widely in the media. Despite the pipelines great effect on our nation, a recent Yale Project on Climate Change Communications poll showed that only 3% of surveyed Americans said they were closely following the project's approval process.[177] 63% of the people surveyed who were aware of the project said that they "strongly support" its approval. On the other hand, only 15% said that they "strongly oppose" its approval.[178]

Keystone Pipeline opponents focus on two key environmental issues. The first issue lies in the construction impact and any potential future pipeline oil leaks on environmentally sensitive areas along the path of the pipeline. Note: the Obama Administration ultimately rejected approval of the pipeline project in January 2012 due to the anticipated negative impact on the environment in and around Nebraska's Sand Hill region. Afterwards, these concerns were partially addressed when pipeline sponsor, TransCanada Pipeline Company, changed the original route to avoid these areas.[179]

The second, more difficult environmental issue centers on greenhouse gas emissions. Let's analyze, precisely, how the Keystone Pipeline relates to greenhouse gas emissions. Tar sands oil is widely referred to as "heavy oil." Essentially, it is "heavy" because it has relatively more carbon atoms than lighter oil. Environmentalists believe that carbon emissions contribute to global warming. Therefore, these people are against importing large volumes of heavy oil into the United States due to concerns that it will contribute to further global warming.

A simple rejection of the project by the Obama Administration, however, will not solve the global warming issue. This Canadian oil will find its way to the American or overseas markets no matter what. If the Keystone Pipeline is not available, the heavy oil will come to the U.S. via trucks and railcars. These trucks and railcars are often more prone to accidents and resulting oil spills. Alternatively, the oil will be exported to other parts of Asia, where it will still impact the global environment. The Keystone Pipeline issue, then, must balance politically stable energy sources and global warming threats.

As of early July 2014, the Obama administration had not yet approved or declined the project. It must be approved by the U.S. State Department in order to move forward. Some commentators speculate that the Obama Administration will choose not to make a decision on the Keystone Pipeline until after the mid-term elections in November 2014.

Natural Gas Storage:

The enormous natural gas supply boom from the shale revolution results in an additional piece of American infrastructure: natural gas storage. Gas storage facilities play a critical role in balancing stable supplies and highly variable demand. Note: supplies are relatively stable, while variable demand changes due to weather and other factors.

Gas storage facilities are generally found in the hundreds of Louisiana and Mississippi salt domes. A salt dome is a vertical deposit of salt that extends from a few hundred feet below the surface to 2,000 or more feet further underground. They are dense salt deposits that can be bored out using high pressure water. These bores create large caverns that allow space for natural gas. Gas is then injected into the salt dome under pressure.

Gulf Coast gas producers utilize natural gas storage facilities to store gas during the low-demand months of the spring and fall (the "shoulder" months). Furthermore, northeastern states offer depleted traditional natural gas fields and fill them with further stored gas. These traditional natural gas fields are increasingly important as Marcellus natural gas production increases. Now, gas producers can store gas locally and release it to meet peak cooling needs in the summer, heating needs in the winter. In 2010, there were 400 storage facilities across the United States.[180]

The shale oil boom has brought a surprising reversal of the gas flow direction in some major oil and natural pipelines across the United States. Recently, the Longhorn Pipeline and the Enbridge Seaway pipelines were reversed. Also, different portions of the Texas to New York Transco Pipeline have been reversed to handle future natural gas shipments.

The Water Commodity:

The United States' pipeline infrastructure was built over decades to transport two valuable commodities: natural gas and oil. Now, there is a third critical commodity: water. Hydraulic Fracturing requires massive amounts of water. The *Washington Post* reports that hydraulic fracturing typically uses about 4.2 million gallons of water per well, enough to supply 42,000 people with water for a day.[181]

One company, Antero Resources, proposes to spend $500 million to construct an 80-mile water pipeline for hydraulic fracturing operations.[182] The company's objective is to transport millions of gallons of water from the Ohio River to drilling operations in Ohio and West Virginia. This intake pipe could remove as much as 4.8 million gallons of water per day.[183]

Part Two:

Climate Change

17

Global Warming: A Pivotal Issue

The battle between shale and renewable energy sources is, as of mid-2014, fully under way. And the United States' ultimate global warming view will impact the relative competitive positions of each sector for years or decades to come. Is global warming a threat to our worldwide economy, regional political stability, and the general health of the global environment?

The stakes could hardly be higher. We Americans could be facing permanently flooded cities around the globe and at home (New York, Miami, Baltimore, San Francisco and New Orleans?), chronic natural disasters (forest fires, draughts and large hurricanes), and humanitarian needs from massive numbers of refugees (millions of poor leaving formerly fertile areas due to draught and crop failure). The particularly insidious part of the climate change threat is that many experts believe that we will soon reach a point where there will be "no turning back" and the globe will not be able to control further increases in global warming.

There are two colossal risks associated with climate change. The first one is, obviously, that America and the rest of the world fail to rise to the occasion and many of the outcomes discussed emerge with catastrophic impacts. The second huge risk is that America spends hundreds of billions or trillions of tax-payer dollars combating global climate change and it ends up being a massive waste or misallocation of resources.

Countless numbers of heated debates by family members across dinner tables, arguments among politicians seeking to be on the correct (or popular) side of the issue and proclamations by the world-renowned climatologist, Rush Limbaugh, have not settled this issue. Neither will this book. What the American public should understand, and this is a little bit ironic, is that the biggest contributor to reduced carbon emissions over the past seven to ten years might very well be the oil and gas industry.

New natural gas supplies from shale formations have significantly reduced greenhouse gas emissions since 2007 (see below). Natural gas has displaced a significant amount of coal in the production of base load electric power. Furthermore, it has helped fuel the space and water heating in commercial buildings, thus displacing fuel oil and electricity—pushing back against greenhouse gas emissions.

Climate change is, of course, incredibly controversial in the United States. American political polarization has allowed little common ground between climate change proponents and opponents. Further problems arise with the wide knowledge gap amongst voters. The guy sitting at the counter at the coffee shop with strong climate change opinions is a great mechanic, sure. But he doesn't have that Masters or PhD in climatology to validate his opinions. However, politicians who proclaim their assurance of climate change may only have their needs in mind: they may benefit from grant funding or gaining political power. It is incredibly difficult to find the truth among the hidden agendas. Who can we trust?

Greenhouse Gases and Fugitive Emissions Explained:

When you burn natural gas (methane), you create carbon dioxide or CO_2. CO_2, as most everyone knows by now, is a key greenhouse gas. There are natural sources of CO_2, like a dead tree rotting in a forest, and manmade sources, like the burning of coal in a power plant. The central issue is whether greenhouse gasses are in fact making the global climate warmer and whether the activities of humans (having hundreds of millions of cars and thousands of coal-fired power plants worldwide) are accelerating this warming trend.

All fossil fuels emit carbon dioxide when they are burned (see table 17-1 below). Even solar and wind sources have impacts on the amount of carbon in the environment. Carbon is also released when solar panels and wind turbines are manufactured. Of course the quantities are far less than those emitted from burning fossil fuels.

The escape of methane from pipelines or production wells, which environmentalists are very concerned about, is referred to as "fugitive emissions." Unburned methane is a very potent greenhouse gas. In fact, methane can be up to 20 times more successful at "trapping heat" than carbon dioxide.[184] Environmentalists proclaim that natural gas is incredibly unsafe and ignore its greenhouse gas reduction (when compared to coal) by about 50%.

Fugitive emissions have two main sources:

1. Drilling for natural gas resources.
2. The large U.S. natural gas pipeline network.

According to the U.S. EPA, methane emissions from U.S. natural gas systems have declined by 10% between 1990 and 2011--even with the natural gas infrastructure expansion. This decline is due to greater operational efficiency, better leak detection, and the use of improved materials and technology.[185] The upshot is that the natural gas industry supplies much cleaner burning fuel than does the coal industry and has reduced their emissions of fugitive methane.

Federal and state regulations monitor fugitive natural gas emissions; the oil and gas industry has responded to this monitoring by widely adopting what are referred to as "green completions." Completion refers to the final stages of drilling an oil and gas well. The United States EPA issued a final set of regulations in April 2012; these regulations target the control and reduction of volatile organic compound emissions (gases that have potentially deleterious health effects). One of these organic compounds was, of course, natural gas.[186] According to the EPA regulations: "For fractured and refractured gas wells, the rule generally requires owners/operators to use reduced emissions completions, also known as 'RECs' or 'green completions' to reduce VOC emissions from well completions.[187] (REC's in this context is not to be confused with Renewable Energy Credits). To achieve these VOC reductions, owners and/or operators may use RECs or completion combustion devices, such as flaring, until January 1, 2015; as of January 1, 2015, owners and/or operators must use RECs and a completion combustion device."[188] The new procedures are green because they involve removing natural gas from the removed water after the hydraulic fracturing process. Without this added step, the gas would be emitted into the environment (fugitive gas), unless flared (resulting in carbon dioxide emissions).

Pushing Our Greenhouse Gas Limitations:

The rate of greenhouse gas growth increase (from all sources) has accelerated in recent years. For example, the scientific center on Mauna Loa in Hawaii recorded an atmospheric level of carbon dioxide of 400 parts per million (PPM) in May 2013.[189] According to the National Geographic Society, this level of concentration was reached "for the first time in 55 years of measurement—and probably more than 3 million years of Earth history."[190]

According to some analysts, 400 PPM is a sort of tipping point for the global environment. In a recent NASA article, Dr. Erika Podest provided the following comments on the 400 PPM threshold:

"CO_2 concentrations haven't been this high in millions of years. Even more alarming is the rate of increase in the last five decades and the fact that CO_2 stays in the atmosphere for hundreds or thousands of years. This milestone is a wake-up call that our actions in response to climate change need to match the persistent rise in CO_2. Climate change is a threat to life on Earth and we can no longer afford to be spectators."[191]

– Dr. Erika Podest, Carbon and water cycle research scientist.

Despite warnings such as those above, the American people could hardly be more ambivalent about climate change. The level of climate change concern can be understood with just a quick glance at Google's search engine function called "trends". United States' search activity is set to an index value of 100 at its peak. A recent search for the term "global warming" on the trends page showed a significant increase in search activity from 2004 (index level of 18 in January 2004) to a peak of 100 in April 2007. Since then, the search activity index for the term has fallen to 14 in June 2014. This 86% drop in search activity shows a sharp fall in interest. Similarly, "climate change" reached a peak of 100 in December 2009 and fell to 27 by August 2014. Also of note: the term "Al Gore" reached a peak of 100 in October 2007 and was at only 7 in June 2014.

What caused this global warming interest rise from January 2004 to its peak in April 2007? As aforementioned, the growing interest in the concept of peak oil had a direct, positive impact on renewable energy and global warming interest in the late 1990's and through 2007. Ironically, a problem within the oil and gas industry ("peak oil") spurred interest in global warming; one solution (the shale energy revolution) contributed to the decline of interest.

Another indication that the American public is not very concerned about climate change was a March 2014 Gallup poll. The results showed that climate change ranked on 14th in a list of issues that the American public is worried about. Climate change came in behind the economy, federal spending, terrorism, drug use, illegal immigration and a host of other issues.[192] Only 24% of respondents said that they worry about climate change "a great deal".

So, why the loss in interest? Well, Americans have also lost confidence in many of our national institutions. This could, perhaps, be traced back to the 1970's Watergate scandal. Furthermore, Wall Street has recently "collapsed" twice (in 2000 and 2009), we have seen two wars (Iraq and Afghanistan) drag on painfully for years, and we have watched our political leaders raise our national debt by more than $10 trillion in recent years. To add insult to injury, sports "heroes" have dropped the ball, and our colleges and universities are charging us fortunes to prepare our children for jobs that seem to no longer lead to prosperous careers. Finally, Y2k, the perceived threat of widespread computer malfunctions as we entered the 21st century turned out to be a complete dud. In this context, we can understand why the American people are reluctant to head down a decades-long global warming warpath that could cost hundreds of billions or trillions of dollars.

One politically popular local way of addressing global warming during the late 1990's to 2006 was for Americans to advocate and vote for Renewable Portfolio Standards (RPS) at the state level. These laws require local utilities to derive a certain percentage of their electricity generation from renewable energy sources. These bills have been quite effective in encouraging the development of renewable energy projects. As of March 2013, 29 states had implemented RPS's, and another 8 states had renewable portfolio goals.[193] RPS's require electric utilities to obtain a certain percentage of energy needs from various renewable energy sources. The standards vary considerably from one state to another; they place emphasis on different energy sources depending on local availability.

Kyoto Protocol:

So, with the United States government providing oversight to the world's largest economy, did they choose to take the lead in fighting climate change? Well, the United States signed the Kyoto Protocol on November 12, 1998, but Congress refused to ratify it.[194] The United States is, however, not the world's largest emitter of carbon dioxide. China is. With a total share of global greenhouse gas emissions of 27% in 2012, versus the United States with 14%, China is the clear leader in threatening the global environment.[195] Under the Kyoto Protocol, however, China and India are not required to cut greenhouse gas emissions.[196] Essentially, these countries are considered developing economies whereas (it is argued) the United States and Europe have benefited economically from their carbon emissions for over 100 years. China has been increasing its carbon emissions in spectacular fashion over the past decade as it builds more coal-fired electric power generation capacity. With the world's two largest emitters of carbon (China and the United States, largest until 2006) not taking part in cutting emissions, it is easy to see why there is little global enthusiasm behind the climate change fight.

United States' Declining Carbon Dioxide Emissions:

According to the United States' EIA, energy-related carbon dioxide emissions declined by 3.8% in 2012.[197] The 2012 decrease continued the trend of lower CO_2 emissions, which were at the lowest level since 1994 and over 12% below the 2007 peak level.[198] Carbon dioxide emissions from energy related activities have fallen through 5 of the last 7 years.[199] This decline is attributable, in large measure, to the advent of the shale energy boom (and growth in renewable energy). This has led to lower natural gas prices and, in turn, to fewer tons of burned coal; a clear win for America.

Although this trend is favorable, the United States and other nations must cut emissions much further to avert the full impact of global climate change. Proposed policies and mechanisms for placing an economic cost on carbon, such as a carbon tax or a "cap and trade system" (where emissions are capped and excess emission capacity is traded), have not garnered the necessary political support. Business interests are concerned that raising the cost of business will simply place us at a comparative disadvantage to other nations, like China, and that the result will be higher costs and job losses. The United States may have historic responsibility for significant carbon emissions. However, the major polluter today, globally and by a wide margin, is China.

The table below provides specific data on the emissions of carbon dioxide, sulfur dioxide, and nitrogen oxides from burning fossil fuels.

Fossil Fuel-Fired Power Plant Emissions: Table 17-1

Generation Fuel Type	Carbon Dioxide (CO2) LB/MWh (1)	Sulfur Dioxide (SO2) LB/MWh	Nitrogen Oxides (NOX) LB/MWh
Coal	2,249	13	6
Natural Gas	1,135	0.1	1.7
Oil	1,672	12	4

Source: "Leveraging Natural Gas to Reduce Greenhouse Gas Emissions" Center for Climate and Energy Solutions, June 2013. (1) Pounds per Megawatt Hour of electric power production.

The emissions of CO_2, SO_2, and NOx for solar, hydroelectric, and wind power are not shown in the table. There are no direct greenhouse gas emissions from wind and solar power production. Of course, wind turbine manufacture utilizes conventional energy. However, this is negligible in comparison to the significant amounts of greenhouse gas emissions avoided through the use of wind or solar power.

Intergovernmental Panel on Climate Change:

An important development in the global warming threat occurred on September 27, 2013. The United Nations Intergovernmental Panel on Climate Change (IPCC) released its Working Group I (WGI) contribution to their Fifth Assessment Report. The IPCC also issued four previous assessments with the first being in 1990 (2nd, 3rd, and 4th in 1996, 2001, and 2007, respectively).[200]

Some of the key findings are summarized below:

- The amounts of carbon dioxide (CO_2), methane, and nitrous oxide have increased to levels unseen in at least the last 800,000 years. Carbon dioxide levels have increased by 40% since the pre-industrial period, primarily from fossil fuel emissions.[201]
- Climate warming is unequivocal, and since the 1950s, many of the observed changes are unprecedented over decades to millennia. The atmosphere and ocean have both gotten warmer, the amounts of snow and ice have declined, sea levels have risen, and the concentrations of greenhouse gases have increased."[202]
- Over the last two decades, the Greenland and Antarctic ice sheets have been losing mass, glaciers have continued to shrink almost worldwide, and Arctic sea ice and Northern Hemisphere spring snow cover have continued to decrease in extent.
- "It is extremely likely that human influence has been the dominant cause of the observed warming since the mid-20th century."

The WGI report was reviewed by 1,089 experts and 38 governments; it generated 54,677 comments.[203] Therefore, this is clearly not the work of a handful of environmental alarmists.

The phrase "extremely likely" in the last bullet point above is defined by the WGI as having a 95% to 100% certainty.[204] Together, these 1,089 experts have, therefore, concluded that, with 95% or more certainty, mankind's activities has caused the observed increase in global warming.[205] This level of certainty (95%-100%) that mankind has caused global warming is the highest since the first report was released in 1990.

Well, if the American public is ambivalent about climate change, what about our President, Barack Obama? Perhaps the one subject more controversial than climate change is the question of the effectiveness and competence of America's 44th President. Some right-wing conservatives in the U.S. describe President Obama as a socialist. Is he following a far left -wing agenda on climate change? Clearly, he has led the fight against coal and his administration has held up approval of the Keystone Pipeline for an inordinate amount of time. Also, his administration negotiated the much higher CAFÉ standards during the automobile industry's restructuring. However, he has also been supportive of oil and gas in some areas and the EPA appears to be somewhat cautious in its attacks on Hydraulic Fracturing (compared to coal, at least). For example, the Administration approved Shell's drilling for oil in the Beaufort Sea in 2012, which was subsequently revoked after Shell experienced technical problems.[206] Nevertheless, opening the Arctic to oil drilling was a major accommodation to the oil and gas industry by the Obama Administration.

As the Obama Administration moves towards its completion, we may see more unilateral action to fight climate change, particularly after the mid-term elections in November 2014. However, the political views and opinions held by the American public, in the aggregate, will have a profound impact on the future growth of renewable energy. A central issue, of course, will be our views on global climate change.

Do we believe that the global climate is changing (getting warmer) and that mankind is contributing to the acceleration of this change? The answer to this critical question will have profound impacts on which politicians we vote for, whether we buy solar panels for our homes, which cars we choose to drive (the enormous, gasoline guzzling SUV or the hybrid) and how actively we will support key state and local issues, like the imposition of renewable energy standards on electric utilities, among many others. The challenge for renewable energy technology developers and political supporters of renewable energy initiatives is that America's families are now more focused on other more parochial issues. Among these are health care costs, lack of income growth, day care (cost and availability), care for aging parents, skyrocketing college tuition, retirement planning and a whole host of other issues that pre-occupy us daily.

Part Three:

Renewable Energy

18

Renewable Energy: The Big Picture

The shale energy revolution has changed nearly every corner of the United States' energy sector. Natural gas prices are low and crude oil is very abundant. The oil and gas industry is firing on all cylinders. Coal is on the ropes and nuclear power is stuck in neutral. How then, can one argue that renewable energy has a viable future that amounts to more than being just a small niche market? The remainder of the book is dedicated to making this argument. Specifically, a case can be made that renewable energy is potentially (yes, a little bit of hedging here) the source of the America's next energy revolution.

What are the impediments standing in the way of wind and solar each reaching grid parity, on a widespread basis across the United States? The chapters that follow outline a wide range of issues that will impact future growth of renewable energy. These include tax incentive policy, renewable portfolio standards, competition with China, competing cost structures (levelized costs of energy), power transmission capacity, development of potential new power storage technologies, job growth, access to financial capital as well as shifts in public opinion on clean energy and global climate change.

Has the shale energy revolution created a challenging environment for renewable energy growth in the United States? Indeed, it has. However, as described below, 2014 and 2015 wind power growth could be strong given the large backlog of projects that qualified for the production tax credit (described in detail below) before it expired. For a few years following 2016, wind power in the United States could face headwinds in the form of continued low natural gas prices. However, the wind industry continues to lower costs and makes further progress toward grid parity. Solar power, however, seems to be on a more linear and rapid descent towards being able to compete effectively with natural gas and coal in the production of electricity. Once there, the economics of renewable energy will reach a critical inflection point and improve considerably.

Even today, some detractors still argue that renewable energy sources, to some degree, exist only because of past tax incentives. However, re-litigating the merits and prudence of these past tax policy issues is really not terribly productive. However, a few interesting questions that emerge when thinking about the tax incentive issue are the following:

1. Should we allow the United States to fall behind countries like Germany and China who are aggressively subsidizing / investing in their domestic renewable energy sectors?
2. Could we have reached this point, where we are perhaps only a few years from grid parity for both wind and solar power, without past tax incentive policies?
3. Could we have been so certain that climate change was not a threat that we could have confidently avoided building a base of zero-carbon energy sources over the past decade or so?
4. If tax incentives are so repugnant, are we Americans ready to eliminate them for grain, corn and dairy farmers, and banks, just to name a few beneficiaries? Perhaps Congress should repeal the deductibility of mortgage interest or eliminate below-market interest rates on student loans.
5. Can you imagine the amount of energy research that could have been completed with the $1.0 trillion dollars that was spent on the war in Iraq? (At $50,000 per home, we could have installed solar panels on 10 million homes for $500 billion and spent the other $500 billion on basic energy research, for example.)

The above questions are not meant to advocate for eliminating student loans or the giving away of free solar systems. Instead, it is to put into perspective the arguments that some anti-renewable energy pundits put forward, many of whom hyperventilate about how outrageous and anti-American tax incentives are while they are benefiting from many others. As suggested above, however, the renewable energy sector should move beyond tax incentives as quickly as feasibly possible.

Many everyday citizens, news reporters, Wall Street analysts and politicians seem to lump all renewable energy sources together. They have treated them as one, monolithic whole. This may have been the appropriate conceptual framework in the past. Is this still the correct way to be thinking about renewable energy in 2014 and beyond? The renewable energy dynamics are changing quickly. Solar and wind, in particular, should probably no longer be lumped together when discussing their respective outlooks and prospects. Solar is rapidly reaching grid parity in many high- electricity-cost areas of the United States. Wind power may well take a little longer to reach grid parity, but the industry continues to innovate, drive down costs and build ever larger and more efficient wind turbines.

A key theme going forward, both for conventional and renewable energy alike, is innovation. Innovation is not going to stop. Thousands of small and large companies, as well as university research teams, across the United States are continuing to push the renewable energy innovation envelope. Every day it seems, a new announcement is being made about some new type of solar cell technology that raises the critically important efficiency metric, a larger and more efficient wind turbine, or a new type of energy storage technology. Companies like Makani Power and Lightsail Energy, just to name a couple, are moving the ball down the field towards greater renewable energy use every single day.

Two critically important drivers of future renewable energy growth in the United States, in addition to innovation, will be access to capital and the American public's desire for and commitment to clean energy. Financial capital is, of course, the grease that will help propel the renewable energy sector forward. Unfortunately, the Great Recession and the subsequent uncertainty around tax incentives, which started in 2009, had a real cooling effect on the amount and growth in project financing available to developers of renewable energy projects. The challenge now is to be able to attract capital to the sector from all sources, including private equity, venture capital, bank financing, public equity capital (through IPO's) and even angel capital for the next great companies being developed in garages across America. This issue is discussed in more detail in Chapter 24.

Is the looming climate change threat (rising seas, deluged cities, trillions of dollars in costs globally and millions of refugees, in a dire scenario), necessary to ensure that renewable energy will grow substantially in the years ahead? As renewable energy sources are some of the key zero carbon sources of energy (ignoring manufacturing related releases of carbon, for a moment), alongside nuclear power, more tangible evidence would obviously argue for more wind, solar and hydro-electric power.

Suppose for a moment that the validity of the climate change threat is not resolved for ten to twenty more years. Can a case still be made that renewable energy is still viable? Yes, the "glide path" towards grid parity might take a few years longer, but once grid parity is reached, we should see a significant acceleration of growth, particularly for solar energy.

Environmental groups, who are generally allied with renewable energy producers, have seen the enormous market share gains made by clean-burning natural gas (relative to coal) over the past few years and are understandably alarmed. Combine this with America's apparent lack of interest in climate change, and they become even more alarmed. Environmentalists want more wind and solar, not more natural gas.

Unfortunately, the environmentalist's strategy of "knee capping" natural gas and oil production by attacking the use of hydraulic fracturing is just not going to make more than a marginal difference in slowing the production of clean natural gas (and less clean oil). Texas, North Dakota and Pennsylvania are the 800 pound gorillas of America's shale energy industry, and barring some major environmental disaster, they are very likely not going to stop using hydraulic fracturing.

So, how will America's renewable energy sector maintain its momentum and growth? It should focus like a laser on cost control and innovation. Sound like an obvious and basic strategy? Enormous human challenges usually have simple strategies. Think of the D-Day invasion of Normandy. It is the execution of these strategies that is difficult. Renewable energy manufacturers and developers must push ever harder. They must produce solar panels with greater efficiencies, manufacture larger wind turbines, reduce balance of systems costs (racks, inverters, etc.) and hire the best engineers and researchers. Ironically, the cost of core materials like steel, aluminum and concrete, as well as shipping, should be reduced due to the lower natural gas prices caused by the shale energy revolution.

Two key wild cards, which are not related to hydraulic fracturing or climate change that could dramatically boost renewable energy growth are passage of the MLP Parity Act, which allows renewable energy companies to form Master Limited Partnerships, and advances in energy storage. These are discussed more fully in the following chapters.

Renewable energy detractors often seem to view the American energy markets as a zero-sum game. Their idea is: "Well, we have more than enough natural gas, so let's just forget about renewable energy". This is not the correct approach. Instead, our view should be that if wind and solar continue their growth and supply more of our electric power, then great. We can export more natural gas. Alternatively, let's use natural gas to power our cars and export crude oil (our laws prohibiting crude oil exports should be repealed). Maybe we can further cut our coal use, which is very polluting, regardless of whether climate change is a real threat. The best strategy is one that recognizes that more energy is always better for the United States, for our people and our economy.

19

Myths and Reality: Renewable Energy

Before launching into a description of the various renewable energy technologies, it is important to clear the air of some of the more common myths that continue to plague the sector. Some of these are as follows:

Myth: The death of Solyndra proves that renewable energy is not viable.

Reality: Solyndra has, unfortunately, become the poster child for failed clean energy investment by the United States government. However, the truth is not nearly so simple—it cannot be simplified to a bumper sticker-sized tag on a nightly news segment. The considerations supporting the government's investment in Solyndra and the factors involved in its ultimate demise are complex. A full analysis of Solyndra's doom requires its own book. However, we must understand that the failure of a single solar company serving a niche market should not justify condemning the remaining thousands of companies in the renewable energy sector.

The bigger and more important issue of the Federal Government renewable energy "investments" (loan guarantees), however, tells an interesting story. The Department of Energy has a $3.4 billion loan guarantee portfolio to solar wind, nuclear, and other companies.[207] The Energy Secretary reported in May 2013 that only about 2% of the portfolio represents losses.[208] Therefore, although legitimate arguments might exist against U.S. investments in some renewable energy technologies, this portfolio shows no massive failure.

Evaluating United States' energy investment policies requires consideration of the scale of investments required to commercialize new technologies and the strategies followed by our biggest economic competitor: China. The United States Department of Energy, for example, committed to two new electric car companies: Fisker and Tesla. Fisker, unfortunately, was an abject failure. Tesla Motors, however, has been a dramatic success. Each company required capital amounting to hundreds of millions of dollars of debt and equity. Car companies, like energy companies, are highly capital intensive. Oftentimes, single venture capitalist firms or syndicates do not have the capital necessary to reach the scale necessary to carry some new technologies to commercial success. This is where the U.S. government can get involved constructively.

Tesla, led by Elon Musk, has become a viable 4th American car company in just ten years; it is expected to start exporting cars in 2014. Most noteworthy, on Wednesday, May 22nd, 2013, Tesla repaid the entire balance of its $451.8 million Department of Energy loan—thus demonstrating its independent financial strength.[209] This was a full 9 years ahead of schedule. The repayment funds were part of a successful $1.0 billion common stock issue and convertible loans completed during just the previous week.[210]

Myth: Renewable energy can't compete with natural gas without subsidies.

Reality: Historically, this has been true. However, as discussed at length in later chapters, wind and solar are on a clear path toward developing the ability to compete with natural gas over the next five to eight years.

Myth: Wind and solar make the electric grid unstable.

Reality: What, precisely, does this allegation mean? Essentially, wind and solar power are not dispatchable. Therefore, they produce energy only when the wind blows and the sun shines. They must be "backed up" by natural gas generation, making the grid unstable.

This allegation is only true to an extent. Furthermore, the problems were much more prevalent a few years ago when coal usage was rampant. For example, when a 100 MW solar project is not producing power at night, a utility will need a gas-fired plant to provide power for a few hours. When utilities were using more coal-fired generation, this was incredibly difficult. Coal plants are difficult and expensive to ramp up and down (like pressing and easing off the accelerator in your car), even to a minor degree. Also, emissions increase with coal ramping. In the years ahead, however, natural gas-fired turbines will back up solar and wind; natural gas-fired turbines ramp up and down more efficiently. They have much lower emissions than coal.

Also, we must remember that even coal and nuclear plants have back up intermediate gas generators. This is because coal and nuclear plants don't ramp up and down very effectively. Furthermore, natural gas peaking plants (that produce electricity) "back up" base load and intermediate plants at times of peak electricity use. Therefore, this "back up" technique is utilized everywhere.

20

Tax Incentives:
Let the Screaming Begin

Production Tax Credit:

The Production Tax Credit (PTC) is available to wind power producers (and other sources of renewable energy); the tax credit has been effective encouragement in the growth of United States' wind power since the year 2000. This tax credit, or subsidy as detractors would call it, encouraged energy project developers to build thousands of renewable energy projects. Unfortunately for renewable energy project developers, the political environment has changed.

On January 2nd of 2013, President Obama signed the American Taxpayer Relief Act. The bill extended the availability of the PTC until January 1, 2014.[211] The law incorporated a critical new feature for the PTC. The old law required that 2013 projects must be completed in order to receive the PTC; the new law only required that 2013 projects must begin construction to receive PTC. The law then requires that a qualifying plant must plan to be in service within 2 years. This allows looser, more favorable requirements. Therefore, any projects that began construction before January 1, 2014 will receive the PTC; the PTC amounts to 2.2 cents per kilowatt hour of electric power production for the first 10 years of a plant's operation. The technologies eligible for the PTC include landfill gas, wind, biomass, hydroelectric, geothermal, municipal solid waste, hydrokinetic, tidal energy, wave energy, and ocean thermal.

The U.S. Congress refused to extend the PTC after January 1, 2014. This is a clear setback for many types of renewable energy sources. However, all is not lost. Think of the feature in the 2012 law that required projects to simply begin construction in order to qualify. Wind power industry lobbyists anticipated the lack of political support for the PTC; therefore, they appealed for the "under construction" feature to soften the blow of the PTC expiration. Therefore, there's an incredible backlog of projects that began their construction prior to December 31, 2013. They will find completion in the next few years and qualify for the PTC.

As of early July 2014, the Senate Finance Committee has voted to extend the PTC, but the entire Senate has failed to take up the measure for a vote.[212] Given that mid-term elections will be held in November of this year, it seems unlikely that the PTC will be passed this year.

Energy Investment Tax Credit:

The Energy Investment Tax Credit (ITC) is an alternative to the PTC. The credits equate to 30% of the capital expenditures related to solar, fuel cells, small wind, and PTC-eligible technologies.[213] The tax credit is 10% for geothermal, microturbines, and combined heat and power technologies. Due to the PTC expiration at the end of 2013, wind project developers had to claim the ITC by the end of 2013 as well. The qualification: the projects need to have begun construction in that year rather than completing construction.[214] Unfortunately, the 30% ITC is scheduled to reduce to only 10% for projects in service after December 31, 2016.[215] This places further pressure on all renewable energy technologies to lower their cost structures to be more cost competitive in the years to come.

U.S. Treasury Cash Grant:

Prior to year-end 2011, renewable energy project developers did not have to resort to the PTC. They could instead elect to receive a cash grant from the U.S. Treasury. This program, known as the 1603 cash grant program, offered cash payments to project developers. These cash payments equated to what they could have received via the investment tax credit: 30% of the project's cost.[216] Note: Solar power is not eligible for the PTC, but was eligible for this cash grant program. This program began to assist small wind developers without sufficient income to utilize the PTC and ITC right away. Furthermore, the tax equity market—made up of institutional investors that invest equity in renewable energy projects and receive part of their return in the form of tax credits—was weak after the 2008 economic recession. Therefore, the cash grant gave renewable energy developers an immediate incentive to build new projects. The program created an estimated $26-$44 billion of economic output during the construction of projects that benefited from the cash grant program.[217]

Unfortunately, a number of factors eliminated the 1603 cash grant program. The upcoming 2012 presidential election and the backlash from the high-profile death of Solyndra created a tough political environment. Congress allowed the program to expire on December 31, 2011.

Feed in Tariff:

40 countries worldwide utilize a policy called a Feed in Tariff (FIT).[218] The FIT requires local power companies to buy renewable energy from independent power producers that produce power. The required power purchase price per unit is set out in the FIT. Rates are tied to the cost of electricity production from a source of renewable energy. The FIT program has successfully encouraged rapid renewable energy growth in a number of countries around the world. Germany, for example, has "successfully" used its FIT to encourage significant growth in renewable energy, although as discussed below, they may have been too successful.

American renewable energy proponents have pointed to the "success" in Germany's FIT program, arguing for establishment in the United States. In fact, we tried it—sort of. In the 1980's, some states required electric utilities to offer a form of a FIT called a "standard offer contract". These standard offer contracts complied with the terms of the Public Utility Regulatory Policies Act (PURPA) of 1978. PURPA was meant to encourage non-utility generators to build cogeneration plants (those that generate electric power using a gas turbine and then use the subsequent heat exhaust to create steam for the production of even more electricity). Unlike feed-in-tariffs, Standard Offer Contracts were limited to paying avoided cost rates based on the utility's cost-of-generation rather than FIT's utility cost rates.

A few electric utilities have voluntarily established FITs to encourage the use of renewable energy. This establishment will help utilities meet their state's RPS. Feed-in-tariff rates, however, are typically set above the retail cost of electricity. For example, retail rates might be 10 cents per kilowatt hour, and a state's FIT could be 14 cents per kilowatt hour for solar panel electricity generation. The FIT terms will typically layout the eligible technologies (solar and/or wind, for example), rate and contract tenors (10-20 years), project sizes, sector limitations (commercial, residential, industrial, or a combination), and a ceiling that caps the amount of capacity.[219]

The challenge associated with FIT programs is that there must be the local political will necessary to buy power at above retail rates, which of course will raise utility rates over time (all other factors held constant). Power Purchase Agreements (PPA) combined with renewable portfolio standards, like in the case of Cape Wind, can also result in utilities buying power at above their retail rates. The key difference is that PPA's are negotiated and FIT's offer one fixed price (adjusted over time) that renewable energy project developers know up front.

Germany and FIT:

Germany, the FIT program model, has been successful in raising their country's renewable energy use. Renewable power reached approximately 59% in October 2013.[220] Some would argue that Germany has been too successful. The country, unfortunately, has few oil and gas resources. Since the Fukushima power plant disaster, Germany has been working to decrease its exposure to nuclear power. Their FIT program drawback—an actual advantage to the United States—lies in their high (or above market) power prices. These prices can attract too much investment and generation capacity and eventually drive up the cost of electric power.

Energiewende:

The German government and Chancellor Angela Merkel work toward a major initiative: the Energiewende, or energy revolution. The feed-in-tariff is the core of the program, requiring payment of above market rates for solar, wind, and biogas power. These costs are funded with renewable energy surcharges added to all electric bills. These costs amount to about 5.3 cents per kilowatt hour now and, according to the German government, could rise to about 6.2 cents and 6.5 cents per KWh.[221] This would be an approximate 22% hike. As Germans already pay the highest retail electric rates in Europe, these issues are incredibly sensitive.[222] According to a recent article in Der Spiegel, a leading news magazine in Germany: "This year, German consumers will be forced to pay Euro 20 billion ($26 billion) for electricity from solar, wind, and biogas plants--electricity with a market price of just over Euro 3.0 billion."[223] These renewable energy surcharges also raise social equity issues because they are, effectively, regressive taxes. Regressive taxes hit poor people harder than wealthier families. Furthermore, there are loopholes that exempt certain businesses from these surcharges if they can claim they face tough international competition.[224]

The United States and Germany are each at a cross roads in terms of setting renewable energy growth policies. After keeping renewable energy companies on a bit of a short leash with respect to the PTC, the U.S. Congress seems ready to let the renewable energy companies "leave the nest" and fend for themselves as they begin to compete head-to-head with natural gas. Germany, on the other hand, has been aggressive in encouraging renewable energy technologies through their attractive FIT program. Now, with energy costs spiking, the question is this: must Germany reduce its renewable energy programs due to growing political pressure?

21

Hydroelectricity: The Original Renewable

Many Americans, when we hear the word hydroelectricity, often think of the Hoover Dam. This massive irrigation and electric power project was completed during the depths of the 1930's economic depression. The Hoover Dam stands at 726 feet high and was constructed from 4.4 million cubic yards of concrete. It was a massive civil engineering triumph.[225] Fun fact: 4.4 million cubic yards of concrete is enough concrete to create a standard highway extending from San Francisco to New York City.[226] Imagine undertaking such an enormous project in 2014 without using today's computer technology.

Grand Coulee Dam:

The Grand Coulee Dam one-ups the Hoover Dam, however, with 6,809 MW of electric generating capacity versus Hoover Dam's 2,080 MW.[227] Let's put this 6,809 MW number into perspective: the largest wind farm in the United States, the Alta Wind Farm in Kern County, California, has a capacity of just 1,020 MW. As large as this wind project is, it is less than 1/6th the size of the Grand Coulee Dam.[228]

Hydroelectric Versus Other Sources:

Total renewable energy supplied 12% of American electric power in 2012.[229] 56% of this renewable energy was supplied from hydropower. Therefore, 6.7% of the total American electric power was hydroelectric.[230]

Hydropower has some key advantages. It has low marginal cost, operating flexibility as the power generation can readily be ramped up and down, and virtually no greenhouse gas emissions after start-up. In one sense, hydroelectric power is a form of solar power. Solar heating and evaporation bring the water that "fuels" hydropower.

Hydropower, like all energy sources, does have its own drawbacks. Chief among these are environmental impact concerns. There are three kinds of hydroelectric projects, and each has its own general level of environmental impacts. These three kinds are hydroelectric dams, run of river systems, and small/micro hydro. The largest hydroelectric dams are those like Grand Coulee and Hoover Dams. Run of river dams do not create massive reservoirs; instead they use a fixed structure and the river's current to turn turbines. Small/micro hydro impact the environment the least.

Private and publicly owned (other than the federal government) hydroelectric plants are regulated and must be licensed by the Federal Energy Regulatory Commission (FERC). 50% of the America's hydroelectric plants are not owned by the federal government and are therefore subject to FERC regulation.[231]

The early 20th century United States saw the enormous potential of its rivers to power the country's massive economic growth. This promise of cheap abundant power brought the building of thousands of dams in the first half of the twentieth century. By the 1940's, hydropower supplied approximately 75% of the electricity used in the West and Northwest; overall, it supplied about 33% of the United States' total power.[232]

The Distrust of Hydroelectric Power:

Due to decades of environmental activism, however, dams are now being dismantled and removed. For example, the Edwards hydroelectric dam on Augusta, Maine's Kennebec River was demolished and removed in 1999.[233] The dam included a tiny hydropower plant with only 3.5 MW of generating capacity.[234] However, the plant's destruction marked the first time that the FERC had ordered the removal of a hydropower plant against its owner's wishes.[235]

Alaskan Susitna-Watana Hydro Project:

Alaska, however, is bucking this elimination trend. The Alaska Energy Authority has drawn up plans to build a large, new hydroelectric plant, known as the Susitna-Watana Hydro project. This is not just a modest, local project. At 735 feet in height with total generating capacity of 600 MW and a cost of $5.2 billion, this project could provide power to two thirds of Alaska's residents.[236] Located about 185 miles up the Susitna River from Cook Inlet, the project lies between two of Alaska's major cities: Fairbanks and Anchorage. The subsequent reservoir would be about 42 miles long and 1 mile wide.[237] The plans are for the project to come online in 2024.

The project's potential negative environmental impacts are currently under evaluation. Researchers are studying impacts to geology, soils, water resources, fish, aquatic resources, wildlife resources, botanical impacts, recreation, aesthetic changes, and socioeconomic effects. The project could bring numerous benefits as well, boosting future cost competition in electric power. Furthermore, the Susitna-Watana renewable project will assist Alaska in reaching its goal of generating 50% of its electric power from renewable power by 2025. This project could stand as a precedent for future hydroelectric projects nationwide.

Alaska's Natural Gas Resources:

Alaska provides a heated battleground between natural gas and renewable energy. Historically, Alaska has been well endowed with oil and natural gas resources. Now, however, the state must decide between developing large natural gas or hydropower projects. They could, of course, decide to develop both. Natural gas is incredibly abundant on Alaska's North Slope. Much of the North Slope's natural gas is re-injected into oil reservoirs to enhance the production of oil. The North Slope is an enormous natural gas resource, amounting to a total of about 35 TCF, equal to about 1.4x American annual gas consumption.[238]

ExxonMobil has proposed a natural gas pipeline that would extend from the North Slope past Fairbanks to the Anchorage and Cook Inlet area. A new LNG liquefaction plant would be built in Nikiski, Alaska, and LNG would be exported to markets in the United States and Asia. This pipeline and LNG facility are known as the South Central LNG project (SCLNG). A portion of this proposed natural gas transported south by pipeline could be diverted to fuel electric power plants around the Fairbanks and Anchorage areas, as well. This would provide relatively clean energy needed in this area of Alaska.

Alaska has a great task before it. Should it pursue one or both of these large energy projects? Each project, the SCLNG project and the Susitna-Watana Hydroelectric project, requires large capital commitment. Susitna-Watana requires $5.2 billion, while SCLNG requires $45-65 billon.[239] Direct comparisons of the hydroelectric project and the pipeline project in relation to natural gas capacities are necessary to decide; however, these comparisons are not yet available. Furthermore, each project's state revenues in the form of fees and taxes are critical. A large number of environmental issues for each project will need to be studied prior to going forward.

The Threat to Hydroelectric Power:

Hydroelectric power, unfortunately, is dwindling in the United States. With the large exception of Alaska, no new, major hydroelectric projects have been proposed. Also, many dams have been dismantled. There are, however, still about 2,500 dams that provide 78,000 MW of power capacity.[240] Rather than focusing on building large scale hydroelectric dams from scratch, some in the industry, including the National Hydropower Association, advocate adding turbines and generators to existing non-powered dams (NPD). Approximately 80,000 NPD's exist in the United States.[241]

According to an April 2012 study by the Department of Energy and the Oak Ridge National Laboratory, NPDs generating capacity could add up to 12,000 MW of capacity to the country's electric power plant fleet.[242] Fortunately, 8,000 MW of potential capacity is concentrated in only 100 of the 80,000 NPD's.[243] This potential new source of electric power would, of course, be clean, renewable energy.

The Rest of the World:

All over the world, countries are committing to hydroelectric power projects. China completed the giant, 22,500 MW 3 gorges dam—the world's largest hydro-electric plant.[244] Given the hydro-electric power's strengths and the huge installed base of dam infrastructure across the United States, hydro should be a key element of the future energy policies and strategies.

22

Wind Power: Near Term Adjustments

Wind power project developers across America, turbine manufacturers and others in the industry were successful in increasing America's use of wind energy significantly from 2000 through 2012. Installed wind capacity grew from 2,539 MW in 2000 to 61,100 MW at the end of 2013.[245] This represents a compound annual growth rate of approximately 30.0% per year, which is very impressive for any relatively new energy technology.

Renewable energy detractors argue these successes. They say that the wind industry achieved this success only through "subsidies" and tax benefits. However, it is reasonable that wind power's capital intensity required many years of support before reaching a point where it could compete with fossil fuels without support. These aforementioned tax breaks achieved exactly their intention: the wind sector increased its installed capacity dramatically. This, in turn, encouraged wind turbine manufacturers to hire U.S. workers and build factories across the United States.

The combination of the expiration of the PTC and much lower natural gas prices caused by the shale revolution increased uncertainty across the sector in 2013. Nevertheless, project developers and manufacturers are not standing still. There is still a tremendous amount of work to be completed on wind projects that were started and deemed under construction for the purposes of qualifying for the

PTC before it expired. Going beyond 2014 and 2015, even if the PTC is not extended, there will be continued growth in wind power. This is likely to be driven by state RPS laws, which require electric utilities to use wind power, and continued progress lowering costs, particularly of wind turbines.

Wind power, as with all energy sources, has its advantages and challenges.

Wind Advantages:

- No greenhouse gas emissions.
- Very low operating costs.
- No toxic or radioactive waste.
- Large potential wind resource in the rural Midwest.
- Unlike coal and nuclear, wind farms come online fairly quickly.
- Creates good jobs in rural areas.

Wind Power Challenges:

- Intermittent supply: wind tends to blow at night--not in mid-afternoon when the electric power is in high demand.
- Wind power declines in the summer, when needed most.
- Causes imbalances in the power grid (requires "peakers" or back-up generation).
- Currently needs tax subsidies to be "economical".
- Best U.S. wind resources are located far from major cities.
- Capacity factor is typically only about 35%.

Innovation to make wind power more cost effective will be critical for the viability of the wind power sector of the United States. The innovation has already begun: traditional wind turbine manufacturers increased the size of their turbines over the last decade in order to produce more power per turbine. In just four years, the average rated capacity of wind turbines worldwide rose from 1.6 MW to 1.8 MW: a 12.5% increase.[246]

The U.S. wind industry has faced some powerful and vocal critics in recent years. However, as outlined below, the sector has reached some important milestones in the past decade:

- The wind power sector in the United States installed 1,087 megawatts of wind capacity in 2013.[247]
- Total installed wind generation capacity reached 61,100 MW by the end of 2013.[248]
- Wind-power generation continued its growth in 2013, with total generation of 167,776,000 MWh in 2013, enough to power 15.5 million American homes. [249]
- There were approximately 46,000 wind turbines operating in the United States at the end of 2012.[250]
- The U.S. wind energy supply chain is comprised of 560 wind-related manufacturers located in 43 states.[251]
- General Electric, Siemens and Vestas were America's largest wind turbine manufacturers with 40.0%, 19.0%, and 14.0% of the installed wind power generation capacity, respectively, in 2013.[252]
- Wind generation rose from 11.2 million MWh in 2003 to 140.1 million MWh in 2012, an 11.5-fold increase.[253]
- The five biggest states in terms of new wind generation capacity in 2013 were: California, Kansas, Michigan, Texas, and New York with new capacities of 269 MW, 254 MW, 175 MW, 141 MW, and 84 MW, respectively.[254]

The figures above highlight the significant growth in wind power infrastructure and power capacity across the United States over the past fifteen years. Yes, the industry did receive tax incentives. We cannot deny that these were forces in accelerating the sector's growth. The key issue now, in mid 2014, is this: can the sector make the final push toward grid parity without the benefit of federal tax incentives?

States with Great Wind Capacity:

As of December 31, 2013, the top five states with the most wind capacity installed were:[255]

- Texas (12,355 MW)
- California (5,830 MW)
- Iowa (5,178 MW)
- Illinois (3,568 MW)
- Oregon (3,153 MW)

Texas, a leader in both oil and gas, is also a national leader in wind power. In the 1990's and early 2000's, the Texas business and government leaders decided to adopt a very specific strategy to keep its role as the energy center of the United States. West Texas has a very large area of relatively undeveloped land that remains relatively windy—thus, it adopted wind power.

Capital Costs and Wind Power:

The battle between wind and natural gas generation lies in capital costs. Wind, of course, has no fuel costs; however, wind power technology has high capital costs. This, essentially, is like paying upfront for years of free fuel. Clearly, the wind industry must lower initial capital costs through a wide range of innovation.

An example of wind innovation lies with Makani Power, which was acquired by Google in May 2013.[256] Makani is a startup company with an exciting technology. They build wind turbines that are tethered to the earth (or a fixed structure in the ocean) and float about 1,000 feet above the ground, where winds are stronger and more consistent. They hope to offer their technology as an alternative to offshore wind projects.

The proposed Makani airborne wind turbines (AWT) cost about 50% less than conventional offshore wind turbines. They furthermore generate 50% more energy than conventional turbines and provide better scalability. They have greater wind resources, as well, with more land area available for economic wind power production.[257] This company is developing a technology that will take years to perfect. However, it is the type of technology that could be disruptive and make enormous inroads in reducing the cost of wind power.

Power Transmission and Energy Storage Issues:

The American electric power grid is enormous, a stretch of 200,000 miles of critical infrastructure.[258] The grid transmits power to tens of millions of businesses and homes across the country. The basic grid technology has not changed much over 30-40 years. However, the grid is the nervous system of the power industry and is likely to become much more critical for a number of reasons: 1) wind power development growth requires more transmission capacity; 2) wind and solar power, due to their intermittency, must be balanced against gas and other power generation capacity; 3) grid intelligence will increase as communication technology joins grid technology.

Wind power development faces some key constraints with respect to power transmission capacity. Wind power's greatest challenge lies in the fact that the best wind resources are in remote areas, relatively far from city load centers. Other energy sources can live much closer to these city centers. Boston, for example, relies on the Mystic Power station (1,700 megawatts), an area located very close to downtown Boston. However, Boston's nearest proposed wind project could be Nantucket Sound's Cape Wind project. Unfortunately, this project is too far away to supply power to Boston. The lack of close proximity to large cities is not inherently good or bad. The implication of this fact, however, is that there are areas that require further power transmission expenditures for further wind power development. Power transmission lines require long permitting processes. They are expensive and meet environmental rebuttal via its effects on wildlife habitats. The irony is there: energy sectors must meet environmentalists at every turn.

The "smart grid" is a fascinating, evolving energy technology. It is incredibly user-friendly: soon, every American energy consumer will know how much energy each appliance and electric device consumes at any given time and on a cumulative basis. The smart grid may eventually harness internet technology to send energy consumption data from millions of homes to electric utilities to better help them manage electric power demand.

Google, a technology mover and shaker, may emerge as the leader in smart grid technology. They're currently moving forward. On January 13, 2014, Google announced its acquisition of Nest Labs, Inc. for $3.2 billion in cash. Nest Labs is an innovative developer and manufacturer of state-of-the-art home thermostats.[259] Would anyone want to bet against Google and their ability to bring innovation to the home energy management arena?

One of the more ambitious goals of the renewable energy sector in the United States has been the attempted development and commercialization of grid-scale energy storage. Companies and universities have worked on energy storage projects for years. Safe, reliable, and economical energy storage would be a significant boon to wind and solar power use. This is not only true at the grid scale, but also at the local and micro-grid level. The not-so-distant future brings Americans "off the grid" because their apartment buildings or individual suburban homes can generate solar or wind power and store it for later use when wind and/or solar is not available or not producing at optimal levels. Connecting to the grid and selling excess power to local electric grids is an alternative to this "completely off the grid" mindset. We are not so far from this technology. Already, American homeowners and commercial business owners are using solar power; they only buy power from the local utility as needed and sell back excess power when available (known as net metering). The addition of energy storage would allow these people to skip net metering altogether—perhaps to the point where they could sell their own net, excess power.

Pumped Storage Hydroelectricity:

Pumped Storage Hydroelectricity (PSH) is an older, well-tested energy-storage technology. According to a March 2011 article in the

Economist magazine, "PSH accounts for more than 99% of bulk storage capacity worldwide: around 127,000 MW, according to the Electric Power Research Institute (EPRI), the research arm of America's power utilities."[260] The PSH approach to energy storage is both simple and elegant. Water is pumped from a low elevation water source up to a higher elevation water storage facility at night when electricity prices are low. The following morning, when electricity prices are high, water is released to fall and turn a number of turbines to generate electricity. The power produced is then sold at a price higher than what was required to pump the water. The drawbacks surrounding pumped storage include relatively high capital costs and environmental opposition.

Energy Storage and the Globe:

The global ramifications of cost-effective energy storage and development could dramatically change the lives of an astounding number of people. As of 2010, 1.3 billion people worldwide did not have access to electric power.[261] 1.3 billion is a number roughly four times the population of the United States; all of those people have no electricity access. Imagine that. Running with our current electricity landscape, the McKinsey Global Institute estimates that $12.2 trillion will be spent on electric power infrastructure through the year 2030.[262] Imagine the billions of dollars saved if wind and solar power was stored and delivered when needed by families and businesses on every continent.

Let's imagine a personal life. A mother of three children in a remote village in Guatemala is kept in the dark, unable to study, or access the internet because she has no real access to electricity. With energy storage technology and innovation, however, this woman and her children could connect to the microgrid in order to access solar panels and energy storage. The knowledge gap could begin to close; this woman and her children could join the rest of the world in having basic lighting services and accessing all of mankind's knowledge on the internet.

Lightsail Energy:

A startup company, Lightsail Energy, has one of the many teams working on energy storage. Other energy storage innovators focus on enhancing various types of existing battery technologies. As a result, significant improvements have occurred with battery technology over the past twenty years. However, LightSail's technology focuses on using compressed air as a medium for storing energy. The company is certainly not the only player in this space. Others include General Compression and SustainX. However, Lightsail is backed by a particularly strong group of investors.

Founded in 2009, Lightsail has raised venture capital funding from Bill Gates and the renowned venture capitalist, Vinod Khosla.[263] Furthermore—and most interestingly--Total Ventures, the venture capital arm of the large, French oil and gas company Total S.A., invested in the company's series D financing in 2013.[264] Also, one of the co-founders of Lightsail, Chief Scientist Danielle Fong entered college at 12 years of age and entered Princeton's Physics PhD program at only 17. Clearly, she's a force of sheer intellectual brilliance and her efforts are being closely watched by the wider energy storage and renewable energy communities.

Lightsail Energy's basic assertion is compelling one: "If it were less expensive to store and deliver low-cost, off-peak energy on demand than it is to make more of it with conventional peaker plants, the energy landscape would change dramatically." [265] The company has a lot more work to do. However, it is clearly one to watch.

Compressed Air Energy Storage:

Navigant Research's August 2013 report forecasts that more than 11 gigawatts of Compressed Air Energy Storage (CAES) capacity will be installed worldwide from 2013 to 2023.[266] A real benefit of CAES technology is its scalability. Storage facilities could theoretically be formed from facilities like abandoned mineshafts or places in the shape and size of underground salt domes. This would make them scalable as needed by companies, real estate developments, and a wide range of other users.

Energy storage would work well for both renewable energy and the electric utility industry. Natural gas-fired plants that normally provide back-up for renewable energy sources would no longer be necessary. Also, hot weather electricity spikes requiring peaker plant capacity could greatly decrease.

Widespread energy storage asks whether we need a centralized electric power grid fed by state-regulated, monopolistic electric utilities. Perhaps the United States could find its power from thousands of independent power producers. Widespread, inexpensive energy storage would strike a major blow to the business models of conventional electric utility companies.

Cape Wind: A Battle for Offshore Wind:

Offshore wind power could be a tremendous source of energy for the United States in the intermediate to long term. Current capital costs for offshore wind projects are currently high; however, advantages of offshore wind argue for a long term, even if limited, commitment to the sector.

Let's look at a current offshore controversy. The Cape Wind project lies off the coast of Massachusetts. Its development is incredibly controversial. Massachusetts, one of the more politically liberal states in the United States (and original home to your writer), is very supportive in development of renewable energy. The project, developed by Cape Wind Associates, is expected to cost $2.5 billion.[267] The project is designed to have 130, 3.6 megawatt wind turbines manufactured by Siemens Wind Energy (a leading wind turbine manufacturer headquartered in Germany).[268] The Cape Wind project is the brainchild of Jim Gordon, a successful Boston-area energy entrepreneur. Gordon's company, Energy Management Inc., developed a number of electric power plants throughout New England (mostly natural gas-fired) in the 1980's and 1990's. After the sale of his power plants in 2001, Gordon turned his attention to developing the United States' first offshore wind project. Cape Wind is expected to generate up to 75% of the electricity needed to power Nantucket, Martha's Vineyard, and parts of Cape Cod.[269]

(As an aside, Jim Gordon appears to be the kind of risk taking, visionary entrepreneur that we Americans should applaud. He has built successful businesses and has staked his own capital and reputation on developing a new and potentially huge source of energy for America. The fact that the shale revolution has pushed down natural gas prices and hurt the economics of the wind sector (at least in the short term), which few if any people could have foreseen in 2002, should not diminish the assessment of the contribution he has made in this groundbreaking project.)

The controversy lies in its geographic location. The Cape Wind project is in the center of Nantucket Sound, an area bounded by Nantucket Island, Martha's Vineyard, and the southern coast of Cape Cod, Massachusetts. This is some of the most beautiful seashore in New England. The area is made up of rocky shoals, sandy beaches with lighthouses punctuating the land, and lobster boats rising and falling with the ocean swells. The aroma of the salt air is everywhere and makes you think of the whaling ships that trolled these waters from their Nantucket Island ports more than 200 years ago.

Some of the wealthiest American liberals who generally support renewable energy live near or have homes on Nantucket, Martha's Vineyard, or Cape Cod. These liberals include the late Senator Ted Kennedy, Joseph Kennedy II, and John Kerry. The core problem with Cape Wind is the following: these wealthy residents will be able to see the offshore wind turbines on the horizon from their summer homes. Apparently, these wealthy families believe that renewable energy is a great idea for places like North Dakota, Iowa, and West Texas—not the middle of Nantucket Sound.

The financial support for "Save Our Sound"—the group against Cape Wind—comes from William I. Koch. Koch is the son of Fred Koch, the founder of Koch Industries—the second largest private company in the United States. William Koch is not involved in Koch Industries, but instead owns his own firm: Oxbow Group. The firm is involved in petroleum coke and sulfur trading and sales.

The cost of the Cape Wind project's electricity provides a less visible, but perhaps more important issue. Cape Wind has entered into a 15-year PPA for half of the project's electricity output with National Grid, a UK company that owns a large electric utility in Massachusetts. The price under the PPA is 18.7 cents per kilowatt hour, which is about twice the current retail rate for electricity in Massachusetts.[270] Also, as a condition to approval of the NSTAR and Northeast Utilities (two large New England Electric Power Companies) merger in 2012, NSTAR agreed to buy output from 129 MW of capacity from Cape Wind.[271] The initial price under the NSTAR PPA is also 18.7 cents per kilowatt hour.[272] This price is subject to decrease if the project costs fall due to lower than expected construction costs or financing costs. The base price may also increase should the project become ineligible for federal PTC's or Investment Tax Credits (the impact is shared 50%/50% by NSTAR and Cape Wind). Baring changes to the base price due to these contingencies, the base price for the power will escalate by 3.5% annually (unless the commercial operation date is delayed and subject to other contingencies).[273]

Massachusetts Green Communities Act:

In many ways, the Cape Wind project is not economical in today's energy environment. NSTAR and National Grid could obtain cheaper power from natural gas fired plants than from the Cape Wind Project. A reasonable question, then, is: why did National Grid and NSTAR enter into this contract to buy power from Cape Wind? Essentially, we must understand the existence of the Massachusetts Green Communities Act. This act requires Massachusetts' electric utilities to acquire 3% of their electricity supply from renewable generators.[274] Massachusetts voters decided that the project's benefits exceeded the relative high cost of electric power for consumers (families, businesses, hospitals, universities, etc.). The Green Communities Act also doubled the annual increase in the required purchases of renewable energy from .5% to

1.0%.[275] These required purchases started at 4% in 2009 and will rise to 15% in 2020 and 25% in 2030.[276]

The Cape Wind benefits are thus: the low carbon production of power, diversification of energy supplies, displacement of power produced from the Canal Generating Plant in Sandwich, MA, which burns relatively dirty oil, and, perhaps most importantly, the opportunity to be the location of the United States' first offshore wind energy project.

The people's mistrust of wind turbines near their homes is not limited to the Cape Wind project. The controversy has further developed in Falmouth, a beautiful, little seaport on the southern coast of the "Cape" just across the bay from the island of Martha's Vineyard. The two turbines were installed in 2010 at a cost of $10 million.[277] Some families in this small town are claiming that they experience health problems due to two wind turbines located on a municipal property. Some residents claim that the turbine blade noise is causing them to experience severe headaches and loss of sleep, among other adverse effects.

These health-related and property-debasing claims are widespread. Some people have called this "wind turbine syndrome".[278] According to an ABC news report on October 21, 2013, the term was coined in recent years by a Johns-Hopkins trained pediatrician.[279] However, the news report points out that the Wind Turbine Syndrome is not recognized by the Centers for Disease control as an actual medical condition.[280]

Windfall Documentary:

The documentary *Windfall* by Laura Israel outlines another example of local wind opposition.[281] It brings an interesting account of how the families of a small New York town, Meredith, battled for and against the proposed development of a utility-scale wind farm project. Meredith is spread across just 58 square miles in the western foothills of the Catskill Mountains; it contains just 1,529 residents.[282] The town's only source of income had been, generally, agriculture and dairy farming since 1800. [283] Although only 160 miles from New York City, Meredith looks more like a small village in northern Vermont. Evergreen and hardwood trees carpet the side of rolling hills and small farms extend through the valleys. Prominent wind power developers proposed building a wind farm in Meredith and negotiated land leases with a few of the residents—clearly changing their world.[284]

Windfall focuses on the actual and perceived problems associated with the impending wind farm development. These problems included potential lower land values, noise, shadow flicker, and the possible threat to birds. These problems are highly debatable; however, the objective of the film does not seem to be to present a balanced analysis of these "problems." The documentary is, however, effective in showing how small town families and neighbors can be bitterly divided by the competing forces of money, self-interest, morality, and the desire to "do the right thing." It also highlights how decisions are often truly based on emotion rather than cold, fact-based analysis.

Windfall caused quite a stir. The late Roger Ebert, a highly-respected Chicago Sun-Times movie critic, gave it a rating of 3 stars out of four.[285] His review seemed to accept, on an almost wholesale basis, the many questionable arguments against wind turbines and wind farm development. Of course, Ebert was not a wind project developer. However, his review does reflect the issue of well-known "artistic" authorities crossing into highly technical, legal, financial, and engineering areas that are associated with wind project development.

The American Wind Energy Industry Association, an aggressive and seemingly quite effective defender of wind power in the United States, had issues with the documentary and Ebert's review. In an article posted on AWEA's blog "Into the Wind," the VP for Public Affairs is quoted as follows: "It was disappointing to see such a normally clear-eyed film critic taken in by such a fact free and slanted take on wind power."[286]

The proposed wind farm in Meredith, New York was ultimately rejected, and no alternative wind project was subsequently built there. *Windfall*, however, does raise a larger question. Is wind power starting to face overwhelming local opposition? The answer is: no, not necessarily. Wind power, like all energy sources, has its inherent disadvantages and challenges. The AWEA said it well in the same blog post: "No energy source, or human activity for that matter, is completely benign. Regardless of how we decide to power our society, there will be some impacts..."[287]

Wind power is far from over. There is a current 61,100 MW of installed capacity across the United States, and wind represents a significant portion of new power generating capacity added each year.[288] In their favor, wind power projects will operate for 25-30 years and emit no pollution, no carbon dioxide, no nitrous oxides, no sulfur dioxide, and no mercury.

To paraphrase Mark Twain: The reports of the death of wind power in the United States have been greatly exaggerated.

23

Solar: Lighting the Way

Solar power has been around for decades. And despite natural gas' recent intense price competition, solar power is likely to experience high rates of growth in the coming years and make up an increasingly large portion of America's energy portfolio. Its core technology: converting sunlight energy into electricity. This conversion occurs directly using photovoltaics or indirectly using a number of different concentrating solar technologies.

Geographic Location:

At the risk of stating what is likely obvious to even the most casual observer of energy technology, solar power works best in areas that receive a lot of sunlight, like the deserts of California, Arizona, and many parts of Texas. The technical measure of the amount of received sunlight is called "insolation." Insolation is the "rate of delivery of direct solar radiation per unit of horizontal surface."[289] Solar insolation is also called "solar irradiation" and can vary significantly across geographic areas. Insolation is typically measured in kilowatt hours per square meter per day (KWh/M2/day).

California's Mojave Desert, for example, is one of the American regions with the highest insolation, typically in the 5.5 -6.0 KWh/m2/day.[290] Areas of West Texas also have high insolation, leaving Dallas and Houston around average (4.0 -5.0 KWh/M2/day).[291] Interestingly, Florida, because of its cloudy tendencies, has a solar irradiation of only about 3.75 to 4.25 KWh/M2/day.[292]

New Jersey (and a few other states) has developed very effective solar energy resources despite having less attractive solar insolation (compared to Arizona, for example). According to the Solar Energy Industries Association, New Jersey ranks third behind only California and Arizona in cumulative installed solar electric capacity.[293] Interestingly, sunny states Hawaii and Florida only ranked 8th and 10th in cumulative capacity. New Jersey has been very progressive and proactive in implementing policies to encourage solar power development.

The solar power sector in the United States has a promising future. The data below highlight the size and recent growth of the solar energy sector:

- Total installed solar capacity reached 13,000 MW at the end of 2013, enough to power more than 2.2 million average American homes.[294]
- In 2013, there were 140,000 new solar installations across America, bringing the total to 445,000 PV systems in operation.[295]
- Development of solar projects by electric utilities drove much of this growth with 2,847 MW of PV and 410 MW of Concentrating Solar Power installed in 2013.[296]

Actual electric generation, as opposed to generation capacity, rose from 534,000 megawatt hours in 2003 to 4.34 million megawatt hours in 2012, a more than 8-fold increase.[297] This astounding growth is generally due to the following:

- Rapidly declining solar panel prices.
- The federal tax incentives.
- The ability to have small-scale applications.
- The availability of net metering (in some states).

Companies in the upstream solar sector (producers of solar panels) have met several challenges in the period between 2006 and 2013 because their Chinese competitors have flooded the world's markets with cheap solar panels. Of course, this has been very good for solar install-ers and consumers.

Unlike grid-scale technology uniformity of wind power, solar's technology is made up of a range of technologies that are available for large and small solar project developers. The table below offers a brief summary of these technologies:

Solar Power Technologies: Table 23-1

Solar Technology	Details
Photovoltaics (PV)	Solar panels
Concentrating Solar Power (CSP)	Lenses or mirror focusing light beams onto a working fluid that is heated and used to create steam to turn a turbine
Concentrated PV (CPV)	Light concentrated using curved mirrors or lenses and directed onto PV

PV Solar Technology:

PV solar systems are made up of standard, rectangular solar panels—like those you see on rooftops of individual homes and com-mercial buildings. These panels are made up of solar cells—electrical devices that convert the received light energy directly into electricity. This conversion process is called the photoelectric effect. The process was first demonstrated by a French Physicist in 1839. In 1921, Albert Einstein won the Nobel Prize in physics "for his services to Theoretical Physics and especially for his discovery of the law of the photoelectric effect."[298]

CSP Solar Technology:

The CSP category brings a number of technologies used for utility-scale solar project development. The basic idea behind each of these technologies is to concentrate a large amount of sunlight into a small area. For example, sunlight directed from thousands of mirrors onto a water container. The concentrated light then heats up water and is used in a steam turbine to drive a generator to create electricity. These technologies include the parabolic, the concentrating linear Fresnel reflector, the Stirling dish, and solar power tower. Since at least 2010, the CSP sector has been in a fierce competitive battle with basic PV technology. The virtual flooding of the world market with PV panels by Chinese manufacturers has hampered growth in CSP.

Concentrated Photovoltaic, not to be confused with CSP, involves generating electric power directly using the photoelectric effect. Some company technologies vary, but they generally involve using mirrors to focus light onto a solar cell. The basic idea behind CPV is to increase efficiency (the percentage of the light that hits the PV panel that is then converted into electricity) by concentrating light and aiming it at a solar cell. Two of the leading CPV technology developers in recent years were Amonix and SolFocus. The latter went out of business and Amonix laid off about 200 people at its North Las Vegas manufacturing plant in January 2012.[299] However, Amonix appears to be continuing to develop its CPV technology as are other companies in this space. Despite near term tough price competition from basic PV technology, CPV could still one day become an important technology depending on advances in system efficiencies vis-a-vis price.

China and Solar Power:

Since about 2005, China has built huge amounts of solar panel (PV) production capacity; furthermore, it has ramped up exports of low-cost solar panels to the United States. China's panel manufacturing sector has grown quickly. From 2008 through 2013, China's sale proceeds from solar panels grew at an annualized rate of 40.9% and reached a total of $86.79 billion.[300] At the same time, Chinese solar cell output (actual units, not sales revenues) increased 56.2% per year. Total production was estimated to be 16.5 gigawatts in 2013.[301] In 2012, as a result of this overproduction, China had to deal with excess production capacity throughout its domestic solar sector. It faced weak global demand. Finally, the Chinese government issued a policy to limit solar panel production expansion. In fact, Suntech Power Holdings, a Chinese company that was formerly the world's largest solar panel maker, fell into and has since emerged from bankruptcy. It will no longer manufacture solar panels; it will become a distributor.[302]

This rapid rise in solar panel production caused solar panel prices to fall sharply over the past 5 years. The average cost of a completed PV System, like those that would power a home or business, dropped by 15 percent in 2013 to $2.59 / watt.[303] Furthermore, the average price of a solar panel has declined by 60 percent since the beginning of 2011.[304]

Solar Power Scalability:

Solar power's incredible scalability puts it at an advantage over wind power. For example, solar technology can be used economically to power electronics, homes, big box stores, and office complexes. Furthermore, solar can be installed nearer to load centers (compared to wind farms), and solar power is often produced at the same time as peak power demand (in the afternoon). Therefore, solar power can meet the high demand. Also, solar can be used both to generate electricity and heat water.

The top 3 states in solar installations in 2013 were California (2,621 MW), Arizona (421 MW) and North Carolina (335 MW).[305] Sunny states California and Arizona are no surprise. California generally leads the country on many renewable energy initiatives, as well. North Carolina brings quite a surprise, however. [306] North Carolina has a strong RPS standard (12.5% of power must come from renewable or clean sources by 2020), and the state is working away from its dependence on coal and nuclear.[307]

Solar power, of course, is met with several challenges. For example, it is not dispatchable because the sun shines when it wants to, not when the solar is needed. Energy storage, however, as discussed above, will likely solve this problem.

Other challenges facing the solar industry include the following:

- Declining Panel Prices: Declining panel prices have been very favorable to American solar project developers, installers, and homeowners. However, the upstream sector of the United States' solar sector, made up of those companies that manufacture solar panels, have found it very difficult to compete with the Chinese manufacturers. The U.S. federal government has imposed tariffs against Chinese solar panel producers.

- Insufficient Tax Equity: Solar project developers, due to their size, cannot take full advantage of available tax incentives. Therefore, they raise project tax equity from those institutional investors, like big banks, that have tax liabilities and can use the credits generated by solar projects. As discussed in a later chapter, proposals and laws are considered to address these needs.
- Quality Control: There are very real issues and concerns regarding the quality of some sources of solar panels manufactured in China.[308] The production race has led to manufacturing issues and corner cutting.
- Sector Consolidation: Due to the lower prices for solar panels and the global excess in production capacity, many solar panel producers will go out of business. This creates uncertainty as consumers of all types plan for their projects. Also, the capital markets, both public and private, are averse to increased risks and uncertainty. This may make financing for projects that more difficult to obtain.
- Commoditization: In order to compete with Chinese solar panel manufacturers, many companies have had to cut their own manufacturing costs and product prices. Some call this "the race to the bottom." The challenge for future American panel producers will be in differentiating their products and commanding premium pricing in the marketplace.
- Net Metering: Net metering refers to state government policies that enable homeowners and businesses to sell their self-generated excess power to their local electric utility companies. In other words, they become power producers and contribute the power available on the grid. Currently, about 40 states have net metering policies in place.[309] However, the implementation details vary greatly. For example, some policies only apply to customers of

investor-owned utilities while others place limits on capacity, the types of customers that are eligible, and the allocation of renewable energy credits. State policies supporting and implementing net metering are, of course, more beneficial than the alternative lack of net metering. The patchwork quilt of the policies across the 40 states creates a challenge for the solar industry growing solar use. A great web site to view variations among state incentives and policies for renewable energy is www.dsireusa.org.

- Solar Power Grid Integration: This issue centers on the intermittent nature of solar power generation and is discussed further in other chapters.

- Venture Capital Funding: Early-stage financing is critical to commercializing new solar technologies. Of course, new companies in all technology areas often die due to lack of sufficient funds. According to PWC, the global accounting and consulting firm, venture capital funding of solar energy companies in the United States increased 82 percent to $128 million during the 3rd quarter of 2013, as compared to $70.3 million in the same period during 2012.[310] Global solar investment by venture capital firms is only recovering after its 2008 peak. Global venture capital investment in the solar sector fell 74.38 % from $3,872 million in 2008 to $992 million in 2012.[311]

- Increasing Efficiency: Efficiency, in this context, refers to the proportion of the light that hits a solar cell that is converted into electricity. Generally, the upper bound for solar efficiency is 100%. However, for highly technical reasons, silicon-based solar cells have a maximum efficiency of about 29%. Although PV modules have declined in price by a factor of 20 from 1978 to 2008, silicon crystal-based PV modules still have efficiency rates only in the high teens.[312] Some in the industry understand nanotechnology's ability to bring efficiency levels above the Shockley-Queisser limit. Why is all of this important? If the power output of solar cells can be increased (i.e. increased efficiency), solar will be able to "create" more electricity per solar panel. Afterwards, solar will be able to compete with natural gas and coal. Countless corporate and university researchers currently seek higher efficiencies for all types of solar cells and modules: look for future innovation.

The United States' solar sector has enormous growth potential as it approaches grid parity. In fact, once prices for solar power fall below residential rates and then commercial rates, the growth in solar power installations may begin to grow exponentially. There is the very real prospect that over the next 15-20 years, the growth in solar power generating capacity may become a threat to the business models of hundreds of traditional electric utility companies. As thousands, then millions of consumers install solar and go off the grid, there could potentially be a large number of "stranded" fossil fuel-fired generating plants across the U.S.

Another key upside for the United States: As solar increases its market share in producing electricity at home in America, we can work to export more natural gas to the rest of the world. America is well on its way to becoming a global energy behemoth.

24

Renewable Energy: Money and Power

As discussed earlier, the oil and gas industry attracts large amounts of capital, in part because of their use of MLPs. Renewable energy proponents recognize this, as well. They've recently tried to have the U.S. Congress approve a new bill: the Master Limited Partnership Parity Act, which would enable many renewable energy companies to organize themselves as MLPs and derive the same capital attraction benefits. Senator Chris Coons (D-Delaware) and Congressman Ted Poe (R-Texas) introduced the bill, which attempts to "level the playing field" in the competition between natural gas and renewable energy.[313]

MLP boosters believe that passage of the legislation would be a game-changer for the renewable energy industry, attracting additional capital to the sector and enhancing the sector's access to equity.[314] And the boosters are not limited: The MLP Parity Act has been endorsed by the American Wind Energy Association, Third Way, Solar Energy Industries Association, Biomass Power Association, Biotechnology Industry Organization, Ocean Renewable Energy Coalition, American Council on Renewable Energy, Natural Resources Defense Council, Advanced Biofuels Association, Offshore Wind Development Coalition, and the Advanced Ethanol Council.[315]

MLP Parity Bill Challenges:

MLP Parity Bill challenges are both political and technical. The bill appeals to both advocates of lower taxes and clean energy supporters;

however, some Congress members appear to be negotiating for a reduction or elimination of the Production Tax Credit as a condition for supporting this bill. The proposed bill's technical issues have to do with which types of investors will be willing to fund renewable energy master limited partnerships.

Most utility scale solar and wind farms are project financed. Essentially special-purpose vehicles (companies) own these energy projects and the project developers finance them by raising capital from banks and equity investors. Generally speaking, there are two kinds of equity investments in project financed solar and wind farms. The first investment is developer equity; the equity is invested by the wind project developers for their own account. Because renewable project companies often do not have taxable income from ongoing business operations, the project developers require outside investors that can take advantage of the tax incentives (PTCs). These investors are known as "tax equity investors." Historically, these investors are large financial institutions that have ample tax capacity; they are looking for reasonable returns from 5-10 year investments from PTCs.

Traditional MLP investors tend to be retail investors (as opposed to institutional investors, like pension funds); many of these investors seek the steady income of traditional energy assets, like midstream natural gas pipelines. Grid-scale solar and wind projects share many of these characteristics. These projects usually have 25-30 year lives based on both the longevity of the equipment and the tenor of the electric utility power purchase agreements.

As of early July 2014, the MLP Parity Act is stalled in Congress, despite apparent wide, bipartisan support. A June 19, 2014 editorial on the prominent web site TheHill.com by Paul Gaynor, the CEO of First Wind, argues persuasively that passage of the bill would be good for the renewable energy sector, investors and America as a whole.

As with any economic sector, venture capital funding is key to developing new energy technologies. The global energy sector contains thousands of companies; disruptive new technologies are on the horizon, ready to change the world—much like hydraulic fracturing.

Unfortunately, the clean tech sector—the Price Waterhouse Coopers defined "agriculture and bioproducts, energy efficiency, smart grid and energy storage, solar energy, transportation, water and waste management, wind and geothermal, and other renewables," experienced a 20 percent decrease in funding during the 3rd quarter of 2013 from the previous quarter, down to $297 million.[316] Of course, further innovation could bump this funding up at any time.

25

China: The United States' Economic Nemesis

Over the coming years, China will very likely be America's leading economic competitor. By the year 2019, China's economy is expected to surpass America's in size. In order to more effectively compete with China, America must continue to aggressively innovate in all high-value sectors like medicine, internet technologies, manufacturing (thereby resurrecting "Made in America"), automobiles (including hybrid and electric cars) and many other sectors. Underlying the competitiveness of all of these sectors will need to be innovation in both the conventional and renewable energy sectors. Ample supplies of all types of energy sources at competitive prices will be a key economic competitive advantage for America.

The energy sector is one of the key battlefields in this fight for economic supremacy. The following data highlights the enormous role that China has in the energy world.

China is:

- Just behind the United States in rank as the second largest consumer of oil; it is projected to become the largest in 2014.[317]
- The largest producer and consumer of coal in the world; it makes up half of the entire total consumption of coal across the globe.[318]

- The country with the world's estimated highest level of technically recoverable shale natural gas reserves, totaling 1,115 trillion cubic feet.[319]
- Building a rapidly growing petroleum refining sector with throughput capacity rising 113.6% from 4.4 million barrels per day in 2002 to 9.4 million in 2012.[320]
- The world's leading producer of hydroelectric power with 23% of the world's production in 2012.[321]
- Expected to construct and deploy more renewable energy power generation capacity (wind, solar, hydroelectric, and biomass) than Japan, Europe, and the United States combined by 2035.[322]
- Potentially a much larger consumer of energy; their per capita consumption was only 2,029 Kg of oil equivalent in 2011 when compared to the United States, which consumed 7,032 kg of oil per capita.[323]

Americans Voicing Complaints:

The United States' relationship with China across the energy sector is complicated. Both countries compete fiercely in some areas but must cooperate in others. For example, the United States requires low-cost solar panels in order to increase solar capacity. On the other hand, rapidly declining Chinese solar panel prices have pummeled American solar panel manufacturers over the past few years.

In response to this unfortunate situation, seven solar companies—parts of this American upstream solar sector (the panel manufacturers)—filed a trade complaint against the Chinese solar industry in October of 2011.[324] The companies' accusation was that the Chinese panel manufacturers received billions of dollars of government subsidies with the objective of gaining market share in the United States; furthermore, they argued that China had "dumped" panels on the U.S. market at prices below what it cost the Chinese to manufacture and ship them.[325] The amount of money at stake is substantial as China ships approximately $30 billion of solar panels to the West each year.[326]

Six of the seven companies filed anonymously, as is their prerogative under federal rules.[327] Apparently, they were concerned about potential reprisals from Chinese bureaucrats and/or suppliers. The one company that did identify itself in the trade complaint was SolarWorld AG, the U.S. subsidiary of a German Company.

The United States imposed "anti-dumping" tariffs of about 30% on solar panels exported to the U.S. from China.[328] This was after imposing anti-subsidy tariffs ranging from 2.9% to 4.73% on Chinese panels in March of 2012.[329]

These tariffs against Chinese panel producers are very likely justified. However, these tariffs are terribly counterproductive from the standpoint of advancing solar energy use in the United States. Higher panel costs are not what is needed as the solar industry works to reach grid parity to better compete with natural gas. Yes, the tariffs benefit a handful of American panel manufacturers. However, there are tens of thousands of homeowners and businesses (both users of solar and solar panel installers) that are hurt by higher panel prices. Higher panel prices are going to work towards reversing the real recent progress.

Shale Energy and China:

The United States has the upper hand in the development of shale drilling technology. Therefore, we have an immense opportunity to export equipment and license technology to the Chinese. On this shale energy front, China can benefit from the huge potential for relatively clean burning natural gas. As discussed in previous chapters, their air quality is incredibly poor due to coal emissions.

Unfortunately, China does not have enormous natural gas infrastructure, like our interstate gas pipelines, storage facilities, and thousands of miles of gas pipelines. China does not have trading hubs and futures contracts, used for allocating risk among market participants. Furthermore, it doesn't have a well-developed regulatory environment at both the state and federal levels.

These challenges are not causing a stagnant shale-energy China, however. China Petrochemical Corp, known as "Sinopec," acquired a

$2.5 billion ownership interest in five oil and gas fields (four shale plays) in January 2012; they are in current development by Devon Energy.[330] Furthermore, the Chinese National Offshore Oil Company (CNOOC) acquired interests in various shale oil fields from Chesapeake Energy.[331] Their most recent trophy was the $15.1 billion acquisition of Nexen, the Canadian oil and gas company with shale gas and oil sands operations, in addition to conventional oil and gas development.[332]

China and Greenhouse Gas Emissions:

A global issue impacting both the United States and China, these great competitors, is China's impact on greenhouse gas emissions. In 2012, coal's share of China's electric power generation was 67%.[333] Unfortunately, this statistic does not allow comprehension of how massive China's coal sector really is. Bloomberg New Energy Finance predicts that although coal-fired power generation will drop from 67% of total electric power generation in 2012 to 44% in 2030, China will require the addition of, on average, 38,000 megawatts of coal capacity every year through 2022. This means adding about three large coal plants every month.[334] They must do this, of course, to keep up with their massive energy needs.

As of late November 2012, China had plans to construct 363 new coal-fired power plants over the next decade or more. This forms a total generating capacity of 557,938 MW—an average of 1,537 MW per plant.[335] This new coal plant capacity is roughly 9.1 times the entire installed wind capacity in the United States (557,938 MW of China's new coal capacity/61,100 MW of wind generating capacity in the United States = 9.1).

The global pressure against greenhouse gas emissions and the local backlash against the severe pollution in and around major Chinese cities act as a counterweight against this coal production rampage. The United States reduced its greenhouse gas emissions in 2012, but China effectively wiped out our progress by increasing their emissions by more than the American reduction. Total global CO_2 emissions, for example, rose 2.2% in 2012, with China accounting for 70% of this increase.[336]

The United States reduced its CO_2 emissions by 3.7% in 2012; this was largely due to replacing coal with cleaner natural gas.[337]

Massive clouds of smog (a portmanteau of the words smoke and fog) have enveloped major Chinese cities, including Beijing, in recent years. The smog is so bad it can be seen from space. Coal-caused smog is different than Los Angeles car emission smog, for example. It contains more particulate matter. It is especially unhealthy because people are breathing in what is essentially soot and ash. The Chinese wear masks across their mouths and noses to minimize their exposure to outside air. Due to air pollution and the smoking habits of many in China, the country is expected to have one million people suffering from lung cancer by 2025.[338]

China is finally responding. In November 2013, it implemented a policy that prohibits construction of new coal-fired power plants near some of the cities with the worst air quality, including Beijing, Shanghai, and Guangzhou.[339]

Currently, the Chinese are pursuing an alternative to coal involving conversion of coal into synthetic natural gas (SNG).[340] Unfortunately, one study shows that the conversion of coal to SNG results in greenhouse gas emissions 36% to 82% higher than the emissions from burning coal.[341] The SNG advantage is that conversion plants can be located in remote areas and allow gas transportation by pipeline into the cities.

China and Renewable Energy:

Despite its ultimate pollution-spewing activities, China continues to have a critical role in the global development of renewable energy. China had total installed wind generation capacity of 75,324 MW at the end of 2012, more than the installed capacity of Germany, Spain, the UK, and Italy combined (70,500 MW).[342] In comparison, the United States had 61,100 MW of installed capacity.[343] Installed Chinese solar capacity totaled 7,000 MW at the end of 2012 while the United States' amounted to 13,000 MW at the end of 2013.[344]

China's wind and solar power growth plans are incredibly aggressive. Analysts speculate that the Chinese government is boosting demand in the domestic market in response to lower demand in the European and American markets since 2013. China's solar goal is to increase installed solar capacity to 35,000 MW by the end of 2015.[345] This goal, if reached, would represent a staggering 5-fold increase in solar power capacity in only 3 years. China's wind power growth goals are also very ambitious. The country's total installed capacity is projected to reach 150,000 MW by the end of 2015.[346] This is an impressive doubling of capacity in just three years.

Despite these renewable efforts, coal will remain the Tyrannosaurus Rex of Chinese energy production for 20 or more years. Lack of adequate electric power transmission capacity in remote areas, like Mongolia, are already causing curtailments of wind power production capacity due to inadequate local demand. The solar market in China is facing excess capacity (with industry consolidation likely), the need for significant new capital, and import duties from the United States and Europe. Finally, the difficulty and high costs of ramping coal plants up and down are causing problems for solar and wind grid integration.

The world will, of course, benefit from China's aggressive ramp up of wind and solar generation capacity. Increased Chinese production of solar panels and wind turbines on such a large scale will contribute to lower costs around the world. The technology is constantly advancing, and costs will continue to decline. China will, therefore, indirectly help American renewable energy companies compete with American shale gas.

26

Clean Energy: Where are the Jobs?

As mentioned above, the recent explosive growth in shale energy production has caused a very significant increase in jobs. The oil and gas industry, however, has the benefit of a large, pre-existing customer base, an extensive supply chain, and enormous investments in a wide range of infrastructure types (refineries, pipelines, etc.). Therefore, their ability to create thousands of new jobs is not at all surprising.

The wind and solar industries, on the other hand, have several more hurdles.

The wind industry, according to AWEA, employs 80,700 people in development, manufacturing, services, etc. The number of wind-related manufacturing plants at the end of 2012 was 559.[347] The Solar Foundation released a study in November 2012 showing that solar industry employment totaled 119,016 Americans in businesses operating at over 7,800 locations. [348] Note: If these employment numbers are accurate, the United States now has more solar power workers than coal miners; that's 119,016 solar workers versus 92,472 coal miners in 2012.[349]

A leading argument to boost wind and solar power tax credits is that fact that these industries will create new "green jobs". Have the billions of dollars spent on wind and solar related tax subsidies paid the American public a reasonable dividend in the form of new jobs? This is a very difficult question to answer.

Energy sector observers often don't appreciate that once a wind project qualifies for the production tax credit and is placed online, the project continues to get the PTC benefits for the next 10 years. Therefore, there's a constant project pipeline that collects the PTC for each kilowatt hour of energy produced for the remaining number of qualifying years. For example, a project completed in January 2010 would have 7 years of PTC benefits remaining as of January, 2013.

A 2011 Navigant Consulting, Inc. report commissioned by AWEA estimated that extending the PTC for 4 years would cost taxpayers $13.6 billion; however, extending this would result in $25.6 billion of investment over the 4 years from 2013 to 2016.[350] They calculated the return on investment from the PTC extension as 87% (benefits/cost -1).[351]

As with any economic analysis, the Navigant/AWEA study incorporated several assumptions across a wide range of technical and economic variables. These assumptions included the amount of new installed wind capacity, capital costs per installed MW of electric generation capacity, taxes paid on power plant revenue, the number and type of construction jobs, the percentage of turbines made up of American parts, and a whole host of other factors.

Naturally, the PTC extension discussion was as much a political issue as an economic one. The United States hardly has a purely competitive economy. We provide subsidies for dozens of industries and use federal and state tax codes for economic and political ends. For example, the United States' sugar industry has tariffs against Brazilian sugar imports. Even milk is subsidized. However, once the Navigant study was released it was very quickly attacked by a handful of anti-renewable energy organizations.

The other difficult aspect of this analysis is that future employment numbers will increase once the wind and solar sectors reach grid parity. For example, let's say that in 2019, the wind industry can sell power for 10 cents per kWh—with a profit—with the national average retail price at 14 cents per KWh. In this example, wind would be highly attractive, and growth of the sector would likely accelerate—along with construction, permanent jobs, and the building of factories.

27

Shale vs. Renewable Energy: The Holy Grail

The renewable energy and natural gas battle will largely come down to one very simple element: price. We've outlined the advantages and drawbacks of each energy technology, of course. But the electric utility companies remain the biggest energy consumers. And electric utility companies are price sensitive. They must defend their energy source choices to their state public utilities commissions and, ultimately, their ratepayers (who are also voters). With the dramatic fall in natural gas prices in recent years and the limited extension of the federal PTCs, wind, solar, and hydroelectric are on the defensive. Therefore, suppliers must work very hard to make these technologies competitive with natural gas.

Natural gas prices will be very important in determining the future growth of the renewable energy sector in the United States. At the same time, however, it's dangerous to analyze the most recent low natural gas market prices and assume that gas prices will stay this low indefinitely. A range of factors could lead to increased natural gas prices. These are not predictions. They are, instead, factors that could develop over time. These include:

- Growing federal, state, and local regulatory controls on hydraulic fracturing.
- Increasing natural gas demand from industrial customers, including chemicals manufacturing.

- Rising levels of LNG exports (meaning lower domestic supply) due to continued high prices for natural gas in Asia and Europe.
- Increasing use of natural gas for fueling truck and bus fleets (and possibly passenger cars).
- Increased restrictions on coal-fired electric power production, which would drive up demand for natural gas, all other factors remaining unchanged.
- Rapid production decline rates for shale natural gas plays, which could slow future growth of gas production and supplies.
- Some sort of nuclear plant safety issue, which, while not anticipated today, could happen and cause some plants to be taken offline temporarily or even shut down permanently.

Natural gas prices, as outlined, have certainly been volatile over the past 25 years. Because of this volatility, fortunes have been gained and lost by energy companies, individuals, and hedge funds. Any one of the above factors could create upward pressure on gas prices in the years ahead. LNG exports have already been approved, many new chemicals plants are being built, and truck fleets continue to convert to natural gas. Furthermore, permits for new coal-fired power plants are on the decline. Difficult to predict factors in the coming years include potential limitations on hydraulic fracturing and the impact of rapid decline rates on future natural gas production.

Levelized Cost of Energy:

Okay, so renewable energy sources must compete fiercely with natural gas, and primarily on the basis of price. Given that there is no direct cost of fuel associated with wind, solar and hydroelectric power, how does one compare costs of renewable and fossil fuel energy technologies? Well, the primary way is to use cost metric that is known as the Levelized Cost of Energy (LCOE).

LCOE measures the relative cost of producing electric power from different fuel sources, including solar and wind power. LCOE attempts to solve the problem of comparing fossil fuel cost per MWh produced and the solar and wind energies' start-up costs. It is a calculation that takes into account the investment expenditures projected for each year, the operations and maintenance expenditures, and annual fuel expenditures on a per kilowatt hour basis. It incorporates capacity factors (the percentage of time, on average, a power source is producing electricity). These costs are discounted back to the present to take into account the time value of money (for example, a dollar received in 2025 is worth less than a dollar received today). The calculations are often done for periods of 20-30 years. Although the calculation is fairly straightforward conceptually, it does raise issues of which costs ought to be included. For example, should we include the cost of building transmission lines, doing environmental studies, or the research and development done by the turbine manufacturers and solar panel providers?

When assessing LCOEs, we must understand that many states still have Renewable Portfolio Standards. Therefore, some utilities might continue to buy power at rates above their avoided costs (i.e. their own cost of producing electric power) in order to meet their RPS standards requirements. The analysis must evaluate each energy source's potential to compete directly with each other source—taking no PTC and/or RPS into account.

The table below provides summary LCOE estimates from the U.S. Energy Information Administration for a range of electric power technologies. This data is as of April 17, 2014 and applies to generating technologies projected to come online in 2018 (due to the lag time in building new facilities). These numbers are based on national averages. Therefore, remember that regional differences could make a nationally uncompetitive generating technology a very competitive regional technology

Levelized Cost of Energy Estimates: Table 27-1

Electric Power Plant Type	Capacity Factor (%)	Capital Cost ($/MW)	Operating and Main-tenance(1)	Trans-mission In-vestment	Sub-sidy (2)	Total Levelized Cost ($/MWh)
Geothermal	92	34.2	12.2	1.4	-3.4	44.5
Natural Gas -Combined Cycle- Advanced	87	15.7	47.5	1.2		64.4
Natural Gas -Combined Cycle	87	14.3	50.8	1.2		66.3
Wind Power	35	64.1	13.0	3.2		80.3
Hydroelectric	53	72.0	10.5	2.0		84.5
Advanced Nuclear	90	71.4	23.6	1.1	-10.0	86.1
Advanced Combined Cycle with CCS (3)	87	30.3	59.8	1.2		91.3
Conventional Coal	85	60.0	34.5	1.2		95.6
Biomass	83	47.4	54	1.2		102.6
Advanced Combustion Turbine	30	27.3	73	3.4		103.8
IGCC(4)	85	76.1	38.6	1.2		115.9
Solar PV	25	114.5	11.4	4.1	-11.5	118.6
Conventional Combustion Turbine	30	40.2	84.8	3.4		128.4
IGCC with CCS	85	97.8	48.4	1.2		147.4
Wind Offshore	37	175.4	22.8	5.8		204.1
Solar Thermal	20	195.0	42.1	6.0	-19.5	223.6

Source: U.S. Energy Information Administration: (1) Fixed and variable operating and maintenance expense, (2) "Subsidy" refers to tax incentives that will still be available in 2019 (as of the time that this report was produced, the PTC was not in place and is not shown as available in 2019), (3) CCS is Carbon Capture and Storage (This is a way of mitigating the negative effects of emitting carbon dioxide and other greenhouse gases.), and (4) IGCC, or Integrated

Gasification Combined Cycle, is a technology used to gasify coal and convert it to synthesis gas (syngas).

Interestingly, geothermal energy came in with the lowest LCOE of all of the energy technologies. Even without the tax incentives, the LCOE is well below the cost of natural gas generation. Although utility-scale geothermal resources in the United States are limited as compared to solar, wind and hydroelectric, they should be expanded and optimized as much as possible.

We can see a clear natural gas generation leadership compared to most other sources of electricity. However, wind power is the next cheapest source, on average and on a national basis. Furthermore, the cost figures do not include benefits that might result from the Production Tax Credit. Therefore, on a head-to-head basis, wind is not far behind the best natural gas technologies. Wind is, however, still 21.1% more expensive than a simple combined cycle gas plant; therefore the wind turbine manufacturers and project developers have their work cut out for them. Of course, this is an average and there are areas of the country where wind is quite competitive and where RPS requirements make electric utilities less price sensitive.

Solar power costs have decreased continually over the past 5 years; it will likely reach grid parity (versus retail rates) in the next two or three years in numerous additional states. Because solar is more scalable than wind power—therefore, small solar installations can be price competitive while small wind turbines generally cannot—there is a significant likelihood that in 3-4 years the United States will reach a tipping point where solar is competitively priced below retail electric rates in a large number of states. After this point, installed solar could rise dramatically as homeowners, colleges, hospitals, sports stadiums, big box retailers, and shopping malls adopt solar power. Of course, this tipping point will begin in local, state, and regional high- cost electricity markets first; but it will then spread to other parts of the United States as solar continues its "flight path" down the cost curve toward grid parity. Also, generally speaking, solar will reach grid parity first with retail rates, then with commercial rates, and, lastly, with industrial rates.

How does one reconcile the optimistic outlook for solar power outlined above and what is seemingly high LCOE level for Solar shown above? When looking at these LCOE numbers, solar PV seems quite uncompetitive given how much more expensive it is compared to coal, gas, and wind. In fact, Solar PV's average LCOE is 79% higher than the comparable cost of a gas fired combined cycle plant. The key point to keep in mind is that these numbers are averages, and solar has a wide range of values geographically. Think of Arizona or California, which have great solar resources.

The LCOE figures above are stated in dollars per megawatt hour. If one divides them by 1,000 to arrive at costs per kilowatt hour, then they can be compared to the solar costs outlined in the table below. An average LCOE of $118.6 per MWh equates to 11.9 cents per kilowatt hour.

A study released in September 2013 by Deutsche Bank projects that installed solar capacity will rise from the 10,000 MW level reached by mid-2013 to 50,000 MW by 2017.[352] The global commercial and investment bank further predicts that after the solar ITC declines to 10% in 2017, solar will be at or below grid parity in 36 states: a full 72% of the United States.[353]

Deutsche Bank's analysts also evaluated the LCOE's for PV solar across a dozen key states and found solar costs to already be under the average cost of electricity in 9 of them.

Solar Costs versus Average Cost of Electricity: Table 27-2

Solar Costs versus Average Cost of Electricity	Solar Levelized Cost of Energy (cents/KWh) - A	Average Cost of Electricity (cents/KWh)- B	Benefit of Solar (Column B-A)
Arizona	11.0	11.0	0.0
California	12.0	16.0	4.0
Connecticut	15.0	17.0	2.0
Hawaii	12.0	37.0	25.0
Nevada	10.0	12.0	2.0
New Hampshire	15.0	16.0	1.0

Solar Costs versus Average Cost of Electricity	Solar Levelized Cost of Energy (cents/KWh) - A	Average Cost of Electricity (cents/ KWh)- B	Benefit of Solar (Column B-A)
New Jersey	15.0	16.0	1.0
New Mexico	11.0	11.0	0.0
New York	15.0	18.0	3.0
Vermont	16.0	17.0	1.0
Average	**13.2**	**17.1**	**3.9**

Source: Deutsche Bank, CleanTechnica.com, September 2013.

The outlook for renewable energy is actually quite favorable, despite the clear cost challenges they face. Wind power is likely to continue to grow strong and build on its 61,000 MW of installed capacity, hydroelectric has some key characteristics (ability to ramp up and down easily) that makes it attractive (and there are a lot of dams that can be powered relatively cheaply) and solar could grow exponentially after hitting grid parity.

Is oil and gas going away, then, as is hoped for by a wide range of environmentalists? Not in most of our lifetimes. Natural gas, in particular, is a great fuel for all of the reasons explained in previous chapters. However, if the last forty years has taught us anything, it has taught us that natural gas prices do not remain low indefinitely.

The oil and gas industry has paid its dues and then some. Most people don't know about or remember the pain that tens of thousands of families in Texas, Louisiana, Oklahoma and other oil and gas producing states went through in the 1980's due to very low oil prices or the massive layoffs related to industry consolidation in the 1990's. People lost their jobs and their houses and many had to move away and start new careers in different parts of the country. The oil and gas industry fought back hard for years and then, through its innovation, delivered a huge gift to the American people: the shale energy revolution.

Highlighted above, in the LCOE data, is the fact that America has a high quality problem: a large number of competing energy resources. Too much energy is a great problem to have. We should view this portfolio as a basket of strategic options (like an option on a house or a particular high-growth stock). At any given time some of these options will be "in the money" and at other times, they will be "out of the money" (meaning some energy sources are profitable in the short term, whiles others are not –but could be in the longer term). In an uncertain world, we need access to a large number of energy sources.

28

Conclusion:

Innovation: the true story of the shale and renewable energy revolutions. It is the constant wheel pushing America's energy sector ever forward. It has brought us from the dangerous coal mines beneath the earth to the giant oil fields of North Dakota and Texas, to the massive gas resources of Pennsylvania, to the solar panels absorbing energy from the sun, and to the pulsing wind turbines smattering the Midwestern plains. And although its current stance brings us, at once, to the economically desirable shale energy revolution, nothing is true for long. Remember: this book outlines the several times we've projected the past three years in the energy sectors' evolution forward and assumed these conditions would remain unchanged. Energy industry observers have made rash judgments without adequate research and true understanding of innovation. The only thing we know for sure is this: innovation will continue to challenge and change the energy sector. Renewable energy use and demand may reach an inflection point and accelerate in a matter of years, gaining market share against natural gas. And yet, it may only grow at a modest pace. Innovation provides surprise at every corner. Most of all, it provides continued increases in quality of life on this planet. It provides continued understanding of the ways in which we impact the environment, and it pushes the limits of the ways in which we can scrape together adequate resources to feed our endless energy needs.

The shale energy revolution began just a few years ago. Just ten years ago, for example, we were soaking up as much foreign oil as we could. We're currently pausing, understanding where innovation has brought us: to an age of economic stability. To an age of cleaner energy, especially from natural gas. However, because this shale energy revolution began only a few years ago, the battle between shale energy and renewable energy is in its very early stages.

Global warming's effect on both the planet and on the public's opinion could have a huge effect on the renewable energy sector. If public opinion warrants increased renewable energy sector usage—or if global warming rears an undeniably ugly head in the next few years—we could be adopting solar even more rapidly. The thing about global warming is, of course, that it is a huge wildcard. We have no way of entirely predicting what will occur.

The renewable energy sector must make an aggressive, innovative drive over the next ten years and beyond. The path to grid parity lies before us, and the hard work must continue and accelerate. Victories on tax incentives in Congress are no longer enough. Trying to stop hydraulic fracturing is no longer enough; in fact, that ship has sailed. The renewable energy sector must fully adopt an almost singular focus on reducing costs through the entire supply chain, from basic research to the final installation of wind turbines to solar panels. Sound obvious? Yes, but the truth often is. The execution will prove tricky.

We've discussed both sides of the battle between shale and renewable energy, and we've drawn no hard and fast conclusions. It is far too early to declare either side the victor. To do so would be to deny the critical importance of innovation in shaping the future of America's energy economy. With virtually no resolution of the global climate change debate, it is impossible to know the trajectory of future policy issues, regulations, and sources of political pressure to address this potential global threat. However, we understand both sides of America's incredibly dynamic, innovative energy economy. What a vast national resource it is, no?

Of course, the United States' current energy resources—natural gas and oil found all over the country from Pennsylvania to North Dakota to Texas to California—is a huge asset. Not to mention the huge infrastructure needed to deliver the energy. It gives us an extensive leap in terms of world power. We no longer have to lean on Middle Eastern countries; and therefore, we may have a strategic way of getting out of the endless wars that drag on for years. Having our own resources is critically important; it allows us to compete with world power China even as they increase their growth in both their fossil fuels and renewable energy sectors. Most notably, of course, in this equation is the United States' large leap in the shale energy revolution. China must look to us to understand the shale energy revolution. As they creep toward increasing energy importance, we can aggressively pursue an energy strategy that includes both renewable and shale energy resources.

Imagine a future America: a major exporter of both crude oil (assuming export controls are lifted, as they should be) and natural gas, one that is finally fully energy secure, and a country that had the foresight and wisdom to build economically on the base of wind and solar assets. Within ten to fifteen years, America can grow to be the world leader in all major forms of energy.

Endnotes

[1] Reuters. "U.S. surges past Saudis to become world's largest oil supplier – PIRA", October 16 2013, Web, accessed October 30 2013", http://www.reuters.com/article/2013/10/15/us-oil-pira-idUSL1N0I51IX20131015

[2] James L. Smith, Journal of Economic Perspectives (Volume 23, Number 3), "World Oil: Market or Mayhem", Summer 2009, Web, accessed November 30 2013, http://web.mit.edu/ceepr/www/publications/reprints/Reprint_214_WC.pdf

[3] United State Department of Agriculture, Food and Nutrition Service, n.d., Web, accessed May 23 2014, http://www.fns.usda.gov/pd/supplemental-nutrition-assistance-program-snap

[4] Central Intelligence Agency, "The World Factbook" n.d., accessed October 1 2013, https://www.cia.gov/library/publications/the-world-factbook/geos/po.html

[5] Trading Economics, "United States GDP", n.d, accessed November 15, 2013, http://www.tradingeconomics.com/united-states/gdp

[6] Energy Information Administration, "Primary Energy Production by Source, Selected Years, 1949-2011", n.d., accessed December 2 2013, http://www.eia.gov/totalenergy/data/annual/pdf/sec1_7.pdf

[7] Energy Information Administration, "Annual Energy Outlook with Projections to 2040", April 2013, Web, accessed July 23 2013, http://www.eia.gov/forecasts/aeo/pdf/0383(2013).pdf

[8] United States Census Bureau, "State & Country QuickFacts", n.d., accessed October 31 2013, http://quickfacts.census.gov/qfd/states/00000.html

[9] National Atlas of the United States, n.d., accessed December 3 2013, http://www.nationalatlas.gov

[10] Transportation Energy Data Book, Oak Ridge National Laboratory, July 2013, accessed November 1 2013, http://cta.ornl.gov/data/index.shtml

[11] Thom File, Computer and Internet Use in the United States, Population Characteristics, May 2013, Web, Accessed September 21 2013, http://www.census.gov/prod/2013pubs/p20-569.pdf

[12] Rich Karlgaard, Forbes, "What I Learned About Natural Gas from Boone Pickens", April 11 2011, Web, accessed July 11 2013, http://www.forbes.com/sites/richkarlgaard/2011/04/11/what-i-learned-about-natural-gas-from-boone-pickens/2/

[13] CTIA –The Wireless Association, Your Wireless Life, Wireless Quick Facts, November 2013, Web, accessed February 2014, http://www.ctia.org/your-wireless-life/how-wireless-works/wireless-quick-facts

[14] U.S. Freight Cars By Type and Age, January 2011, Web, accessed August 11 2013, http://www.progressiverailroading.com/pr/graphics/pr711statTypeAge.pdf

[15] Fast Facts on U.S. Hospitals, January 2 2014, Web, accessed January 30 2014, http://www.aha.org/research/rc/stat-studies/fast-facts.shtml

[16] Nielson, Nielson Estimates Number of U.S. Television Homes to be 114.7 Million, May 3 2011, Web, accessed November 22 2013, http://www.nielsen.com/us/en/newswire/2011/nielsen-estimates-number-of-u-s-television-homes-to-be-114-7-million.html

[17] American School Bus Council, Environmental Benefits, Fact: You can Go Green by Riding Yellow, n.d., Web, accessed December 12 2013, http://www.americanschoolbuscouncil.org/issues/environmental-benefits

[18] Air Transport World, FAA: U.S. commercial aircraft fleet shrank in 2011, May 12 2012, Web, http://atwonline.com/aircraft-amp-engines/faa-us-commercial-aircraft-fleet-shrank-2011

[19] Ryck Lydecker and Margaret Podlich, Boat Owners Association of the United States, Web, n.d., Web, accessed August 21 2013, http://oceanservice.noaa.gov/websites/retiredsites/natdia_pdf/14boatus.pdf

[20] How Many Motorcycles Are Registered in The U.S., March 15 2012, web, accessed June 12 2013 http://www.howmanyarethere.org/how-many-motorcycles-are-registered-in-the-us/

[21] Recreational Boating Industry, Discover Boating, Quick Facts About PWCS or Personal Watercraft, n.d., Web, accessed September 11 2013, http://www.discoverboating.com/resources/article.aspx?id=543

[22] United States Department of Defense, "About the Department of Defense", n.d., Web, accessed January 17 2014, http://www.defense.gov/about/

[23] YouTube, Defense & Energy Policy Panel at the 2012 Renewable Energy and Energy Efficiency Expo, published July 3 2012, Web, accessed September 15 2013

[24] Ibid.

[25] Ibid.

[26] Ibid.

[27] Encyclopedia Britannica, Shale, August 16 2013, Web, accessed October 12 2013, http://www.britannica.com/EBchecked/topic/538082/Shale

[28] Ibid.

[29] Ibid.

[30] George F. King, Apache Corporation "Hydraulic Fracturing 101: What Every Representative, Environmentalist, Regulator, Reporter, Investor, University Researcher, Neighbor and Engineer Should Know About Estimating Frac Risk and Improving Frac Performance in Unconventional Gas and Oil Wells." SPE International, SPE 152596, 2012, Web, accessed September 23 2013, http://www.kgs.ku.edu/PRS/Fracturing/Frac_Paper_SPE_152596.pdf

[31] Ibid

[32] Sclumberger Corporation, "Completing Shale Plays", n.d., Web, accessed December 29 2013, http://www.slb.com/services/technical_challenges/unconventional_resources/shale_gas_liquids/shale_completions.aspx

[33] U.S. Energy Information Administration, Independent Statistics & Analysis, "Technically Recoverable Shale Oil and Shale Gas Resources: An Assessment of 137 Shale Formations in 41 Countries Outside the United States", June 13 2013, Web, accessed October 12 2013, http://www.eia.gov/analysis/studies/worldshalegas/

[34] U.S. Energy Information Administration, U.S. Petroleum and Other Liquids Supply, Consumption, and Inventories, Short Term Energy Outlook, March 2014, Web, accessed March 2014, http://www.eia.gov/forecasts/steo/tables/pdf/4atab.pdf

[35] U.S. Energy Information Administration, Independent Statistics & Analysis, Natural Gas Consumption by End Use, February 28 2014, Web, accessed March 1 2014, http://www.eia.gov/dnav/ng/ng_cons_sum_dcu_nus_a.htm

[36] Potential Gas Committee, Press Release, Potential Gas Committee Reports Significant Increase in Magnitude of U.S. Natural Gas Resource Base, April 9 2013, Web, accessed December 2 2013, http://potentialgas.org/press-release

[37] Wall Street Journal, Associated Press, "Marcellus Shale gas growing faster than expected", October 23 2013, Web, accessed December 3 2013, http://online.wsj.com/article/AP2e119ea41fcd43248a082bc6e6ad4e24.html

[38] U.S. Energy Information Administration, Independent Statistics & Analysis, Petroleum & Other Liquids, Drilling Productivity Report, June 2014, Web, accessed June 20 2014, http://www.eia.gov/petroleum/drilling/#tabs-summary-2

[39] OPEC, Organization of the Petroleum Exporting Countries, Annual Statistical Bulletin 2013, n.d., Web, accessed October 12 2013, http://www.opec.org/opec_web/static_files_project/media/downloads/publications/ASB2013.pdf

[40] Wall Street Journal, Associated Press, "Marcellus Shale gas growing faster than expected", October 23 2013, Web, accessed December 3 2013, http://online.wsj.com/article/AP2e119ea41fcd43248a082bc6e6ad4e24.html

[41] U.S. Energy Information Administration, Independent Statistics & Analysis, Petroleum & Other Liquids, Drilling Productivity Report, June 2014, Web, accessed June 20 2014, http://www.eia.gov/petroleum/drilling/#tabs-summary-2

[42] OPEC, Organization of the Petroleum Exporting Countries, Annual Statistical Bulletin 2013, n.d., Web, accessed October 12 2013, http://www.opec.org/opec_web/static_files_project/media/downloads/publications/ASB2013.pdf

[43] U.S. Energy Information Administration, Independent Statistics & Analysis, Petroleum & Other Liquids, Drilling Productivity Report, July 10 2014, Web, accessed July 20 2014, http://www.eia.gov/petroleum/drilling/#tabs-summary-2

[44] Railroad Commission of Texas, Eagle Ford Information, March 19 2014, Web, accessed March 25 2013, http://www.rrc.state.tx.us/eagleford/

[45] Ibid.

[46] U.S. Energy Information Administration, Independent Statistics & Analysis, "North Dakota oil production reaches new high in 2012, transported by trucks and railroads", March 18 2013, Web, accessed November 23 2013, http://www.eia.gov/todayinenergy/detail.cfm?id=10411

[47] U.S. Energy Information Administration, Independent Statistics & Analysis, Petroleum & Other Liquids, Drilling Productivity Report, June 2014, Web, accessed June 30 2014, http://www.eia.gov/petroleum/drilling/#tabs-summary-2

[48] Ibid.

[49] American Wind Energy Association, North Dakota Wind Energy, June 7 2013, Web, June 30 2013, http://awea.rd.net/Resources/state.aspx?ItemNumber=5191

[50] Louis Sahagun, The Los Angeles Times, "U.S. officials cut estimate of recoverable Monterey Shale oil by 96%, May 20 2014, Web, accessed May 25 2014, http://www.latimes.com/business/la-fi-oil-20140521-story.html

[51] Ibid.

[52] Ibid.

[53] New York State Museum, New York State Geological Survey, Oil & Gas, n.d., Web, accessed November 23 2013, http://www.nysm.nysed.gov/nysgs/research/oil-gas/index.html

[54] Ibid.

[55] U.S. Energy Information Administration, Independent Statistics & Analysis, Analysis & Projections, "Technically Recoverable Oil and Shale Gas Resources: An Assessment of 137 Shale Formations in 41 Countries Outside the United States", June 10 2013, Web, accessed June 30 2013, http://www.eia.gov/analysis/studies/worldshalegas/

[56] Ibid.

[57] Ibid.

[58] Center for Climate and Energy Solutions, Leveraging Natural Gas to Reduce Greenhouse Gas Emissions, June 2013, Web, accessed July 23 2013, http://www.c2es.org/publications/leveraging-natural-gas-reduce-greenhouse-gas-emissions

[59] Article No Longer available on the NYC web Site: http://www.nyc.gov/html/doh/html/pr2013/pr035-13.shtml

[60] Center for Climate and Energy Solutions, Leveraging Natural Gas to Reduce Greenhouse Gas Emissions, June 2013, Web, accessed July 23 2013, http://www.c2es.org/publications/leveraging-natural-gas-reduce-greenhouse-gas-emissions

[61] Total Corporation E&P Canada, "About Alberta's Oil Sands", n.d., Web, accessed May 1 2014, http://www.total-ep-canada.com/upstream/about_oilsands.asp

[62] Ibid.

[63] Forbes, "30 Under 30: Energy", December 19 2011, Web, accessed July 14 2013, http://www.forbes.com/sites/christopherhelman/2011/12/19/30-under-30-energy/

[64] Ibid.

[65] Ibid.

[66] Sonecon, October 2011, Web, accessed June 10 2014, http://www.whoownsbigoil.org/about/

[67] Forbes, "The World's Biggest Oil Companies", July 16 2012, Web, accessed August 12 2013 http://www.forbes.com/sites/christopherhelman/2012/07/16/the-worlds-25-biggest-oil-companies/

[68] Ibid.

[69] Hess Corporation, Proxy Statement, March 21 2013, Page 32 & 33.

[70] http://www.aflcio.org/Corporate-Watch/CEO-Pay-and-You/100-Highest-Paid-CEOs

[71] Ibid.

[72] AFL CIO, Executive Pay Watch, "Highest Paid CEO's", n.d., Web, accessed November 23 2013, http://www.aflcio.org/Corporate-Watch/CEO-Pay-and-You/100-Highest-Paid-CEOs

[73] Energy Information Administration, Independent Statistics & Analysis, "Frequently Asked Questions", n.d., Web, accessed January 20, 2014, http://www.eia.gov/tools/faqs/faq.cfm?id=29&t=6

[74] Ibid.

[75] BP Statistical Review of World Energy, June 2013, Web, accessed July 31 2013, http://www.bp.com/content/dam/bp/pdf/statistical-review/statistical_review_of_world_energy_2013.pdf

[76] Energy Information Administration, Independent Statistics & Analysis, Environment, "U.S. Energy-Related Carbon Dioxide Emissions 2012", October 21 2013, Web, accessed December 30 2013, http://www.eia.gov/environment/emissions/carbon/

[77] The Free Dictionary, "robber baron", n.d., Web, accessed January 21 2014, http://www.thefreedictionary.com/robber+baron

[78] Forbes, "Oil & Gas Tax Provisions Are Not Subsidies For Big Oil", January 02 2013, Web, accessed July 4 2013, http://www.forbes.com/sites/davidblackmon/2013/01/02/oil-gas-tax-provisions-are-not-subsidies-for-big-oil/

[79] Tory N. Parrish, TRIBLive News, "Two year schools help to fill needs of growing natural gas industry", September 18 2013, Web, accessed September 30 2013 http://triblive.com/news/adminpage/4033481-74/gas-oil-industry#axzz2ezxEm2it

[80] American Chemistry Council, Economics & Statistics Department, "Shale Gas, Competitiveness, and New U.S. Chemical Industry Investment: An Analysis Based on Announced Projects", May 2013, Web, accessed June 13 2013, http://chemistrytoenergy.com/sites/chemistrytoenergy.com/files/shale-gas-full-study.pdf

[81] Energy Information Administration, Independent Statistics & Analysis, "Today in Energy", July 1 2013, Web, accessed July 30 2013, http://www.eia.gov/todayinenergy/detail.cfm?id=11911

[82] Ibid.

[83] Ibid.

[84] International Organization of Motor Vehicle manufacturers, Production Statistics, 2013, Web, accessed March 3 2014, http://www.oica.net/category/production-statistics/

[85] George F. King, Apache Corporation "Hydraulic Fracturing 101: What Every Representative, Environmentalist, Regulator, Reporter, Investor, University Researcher, Neighbor and Engineer Should Know About Estimating Frac Risk and Improving Frac Performance in Unconventional Gas and Oil Wells." SPE International, SPE 152596, 2012, Web, accessed September 23 2013, http://www.kgs.ku.edu/PRS/Fracturing/Frac_Paper_SPE_152596.pdf

[86] Americans Against Fracking, n.d. Web, accessed January 13 2014, http://www.Americansagainstfracking.org.

[87] Artists Against Fracking, n.d., Web, accessed January 12 2014, http://artistsagainstfracking.com

[88] Artists Against Fracking, Video, "Don't Frack My Mother, n.d., Web, accessed November 13 2013, http://artistsagainstfracking.com/dont-frack-my-mother/

[89] Environmental Protection Agency, "Study of the Potential Impacts of Hydraulic Fracturing on Drinking Water Resources" Progress Report, December 2012, Web, accessed July 3 2013, http://nepis.epa.gov

[90] United States Environmental Protection Agency, "Study of the Potential Impacts of Hydraulic Fracturing on Drinking Water Resources Progress Report" December 2012, Web, accessed November 14 2013, http://www2.epa.gov/sites/production/files/documents/hf-progress-report-exec-summary20121214.pdf

[91] Jon Campbell, Albany Bureau, Democrat & Chronicle, "Landowners to sue Cuomo, NY over 'arbitrary' fracking delay", November 12 2013, web, accessed December

2 2013, http://www.democratandchronicle.com/story/news/local/2013/11/12/
landowners-to-sue-cuomo-ny-over-arbitrary-fracking-delay/3506513/

[92] Joint Landowners Coalition of New York, Inc., "JLCNY Complaint Against New York State and Governor Cuomo, n.d., Web, accessed January 5 2014, http://www.jlcny.org/site/index.php/nys-landowner-defense-donation-information/1826-jlcny-complaint-against-new-york-state-and-governor-cuomo

[93] The Journal News, Lohud, Politics on the Hudson, "ICYMI: Cuomo again says fracking will come before Election Day, November 14 2013, Web, accessed December 7 2013, http://polhudson.lohudblogs.com/2013/11/14/icymi-cuomo-again-says-fracking-decision-will-come-before-election-day/

[94] Los Angeles Times, Editorial, "Strict Scrutiny for fracking", November 24 2013, Web, accessed December 26 2013, http://articles.latimes.com/2013/nov/24/opinion/la-ed-fracking-regulations-california-20131124

[95] San Jose Mercury News, Politics & Government, "California releases draft rules for fracking" November 18 2013, Web, accessed December 17 2013, http://www.mercurynews.com/politics-government/ci_24547161/california-releases-draft-rules-fracking

[96] MEDILL, "Take a cross-country tour of U.S. fracking battlegrounds, December 11 2013, Web, accessed December 30 2013, http://news.medill.northwestern.edu/chicago/news.aspx?id=226345

[97] Daniel Wiessner, Reuters, "N.Y. top court says towns can ban fracking", June 30 2014, Web, accessed July 4 2014, http://in.reuters.com/article/2014/06/30/new-york-fracking-decision-idINL2N0P61BT20140630

[98] Organization of the Petroleum Exporting Countries, About Us, "Brief History" n.d., Web, accessed November 21 2013, http://www.opec.org/opec_web/en/about_us/24.htm

[99] APICorp Research, Economic Commentary, Volume 7 No. 8-9, August-September 2012, "Fiscal Breakeven Prices Revisited: What More Could They Tell Us About OPEC Policy Intent, Web, accessed November 22 2013, http://arabenergyclub.com/site/wp-content/uploads/2012/08/Commentary-Vol-7-No-8-9-Aug-Sep-2012.pdf

[100] Ibid.

[101] Ibid.

[102] Bloomberg, Energy, Web, accessed May 26 2014, http://www.bloomberg.com/energy/

[103] Energy Information Administration, Independent Statistics & Analysis, Petroleum & Other Liquids, "U.S. Imports by Country of Origin", September 27 2013, Web, accessed October 23 2013, http://www.eia.gov/dnav/pet/pet_move_impcus_a2_nus_ep00_im0_mBBLpd_a.htm

[104] Ibid.

[105] Ibid.

[106] Ibid.

[107] Center for Climate and Energy Solutions, Leveraging Natural Gas to Reduce Greenhouse Gas Emissions, June 2013, Web, accessed July 23 2013, http://www.c2es.org/publications/leveraging-natural-gas-reduce-greenhouse-gas-emissions

[108] James L. Smith, Journal of Economic Perspectives (Volume 23, Number 3), "World Oil: Market or Mayhem", Summer 2009, Web, accessed November 30 2013, http://web.mit.edu/ceepr/www/publications/reprints/Reprint_214_WC.pdf

[109] Energy Information Administration, Independent Statistics & Analysis, "AEO2014 Early Release Overview", December 16 2013, Web, accessed April 20 2014, http://www.eia.gov/forecasts/aeo/er/early_production.cfm

[110] Ibid.

[111] U.S. National Highway Safety Administration, "Obama Administration Finalizes Historic 54.5 mpg Fuel Efficiency Standards", August 28 2012, Web, accessed September 30 2013, http://www.nhtsa.gov/About+NHTSA/Press+Releases/2012/Obama+Administration+Finalizes+Historic+54.5+mpg+Fuel+Efficiency+Standards

[112] Ibid.

[113] Electric Drive Transportation Association, "Electric Drive Sales Dashboard", n.d., Web, accessed March 23 2014, http://www.electricdrive.org/index.php?ht=d/sp/i/20952/pid/20952

[114] Ibid.

[115] Jason Cammisa, Road & Track, "Return to Power: the 2013 Tesla Model S", February 25 2013, Web, accessed June 13 2013, http://www.roadandtrack.com/car-reviews/road-tests/road-test-2013-tesla-model-s

[116] Chris Martin, Mark Chediak and Ken Wells, BloombergBusinessweek Technology, "Why the U.S. Power Grid's Days Are Numbered", August 22 2013, Web, accessed September 23 2013, http://www.businessweek.com/articles/2013-08-22/homegrown-green-energy-is-making-power-utilities-irrelevant

[117] Mark Del Franco, North American Wind Power, "Big-Name Firms Signal 'Industrial Revolution' For Wind", April 2013, Web, accessed August 13 2013, http://www.nawindpower.com/issues/NAW1304/FEAT_01_Big_Name.html

[118] Ibid.

[119] Ibid.

[120] U.S. Energy Information Administration, Independent Statistics & Analysis, Analysis & Projections, Total Energy, n.d., Web, accessed January 23 2014 http://www.eia.gov/totalenergy/data/annual/showtext.cfm?t=ptb0804a

[121] Ibid.

[122] Alexandra Ochs & Michelle Ray, Worldwatch Institute, Vital Signs, "Nuclear Power Recovers Slightly, But Global Future Uncertain", October 8 2013, Web, accessed November 15 2013, http://vitalsigns.worldwatch.org/vs-trend/nuclear-power-recovers-slightly-global-future-uncertain

[123] Ibid

[124] World Nuclear Association, "Nuclear Power in the United Arab Emirates", January 2014, Web, accessed February 2014, http://www.world-nuclear.org/info/Country-Profiles/Countries-T-Z/United-Arab-Emirates/#.UmFoLtLIHeU

[125] Energy Information Administration, Independent Statistics & Analysis, "Today in Energy", July 2 2013, Web, accessed November 2 2013, http://www.eia.gov/today-inenergy/detail.cfm?id=11931

[126] Ibid.

[127] Ibid.

[128] U.S. Energy Information Administration, "Table 4.1 Count of Electric Power Industry Power Plants, by Sector, by Predominant Energy Sources within Plant, 2002 through 2012", n.d., Web, accessed January 23 2014, http://www.eia.gov/electricity/annual/html/epa_04_01.html

[129] U.S. Energy Information Administration, "Table 5.1.A. Coal: Consumption for Electricity Generation by Sector", n.d., Web, accessed December 13 2013, http://www.eia.gov/electricity/annual/html/epa_05_01_a.html

[130] Ibid.

[131] Center for Climate and Energy Solutions, Leveraging Natural Gas to Reduce Greenhouse Gas Emissions, June 2013, Web, accessed July 23 2013, http://www.c2es.org/publications/leveraging-natural-gas-reduce-greenhouse-gas-emissions

[132]   Michael Wines, New York Times, "E.P.A is Expected to Set Limits on Greenhouse Gas Emissions by New Power Plants", September 13 2013, Web, accessed January 3 2014,   http://www.nytimes.com/2013/09/14/us/epa-is-expected-to-set-limits-on-greenhouse-gas-emissions-by-new-power-plants.html?_r=0

[133]   The Economist, Politics and energy policy, "Appalachian fall", September 28 2013, Web, accessed October 25 2013,   http://www.economist.com/news/united-states/21586897-new-carbon-regulations-will-make-life-harder-still-beleaguered-region-appalachian

[134]   U.S. Department of Labor, Mine Safety & Health Administration, Number of Operator Injuries, January – December 2012, Web, accessed November 23 2013, http://www.msha.gov/STATS/PART50/WQ/2012/table1.pdf

[135]   United States Environmental Protection Agency, Regulatory Actions, "Final Mercury and Air Toxics Standards (MATS) for Power Plants", March 28 2013, Web, accessed December 2 2013, http://www.epa.gov/mats/actions.html

[136]   Ibid.

[137]   United States Environmental Protection Agency, Carbon Pollution Standards, "Clean Power Plan Proposed Rule", June 2 2014, Web, accessed June 30 2014, http://www2.epa.gov/carbon-pollution-standards/clean-power-plan-proposed-rule

[138]   Ibid.

[139]   Ibid.

[140]   Ibid.

[141]   C-SPAN, Carbon Emissions Reduction, Video, June 2 2014, Web, accessed July 3 2014, http://www.c-span.org/video/?319690-1/epa-calls-30-cut-power-plant-emissions

[142]   Cliford Krauss, The New York Times, Energy & Environment, "U.S. Coal Companies Scale Back Export Goals", September 13 2013, Web, accessed January 14 2014,   http://www.nytimes.com/2013/09/14/business/energy-environment/us-coal-companies-scale-back-export-goals.html?_r=0

[143]   Power Engineering, "U.S. coal fired power plants invested more than $30 bn on scrubbers in four years", March 25 2013, Web, accessed June 23 2014, http://www.power-eng.com/articles/2013/03/us-coal-fired-power-plants-invested-more-than-30bn-on-scrubbers-.html

[144]   Gabe Moreen, Derek Walker and Kathleen Morris, Bank of America Merrill Lynch Equity Research, "Energy MLPs: Monthly sector presentation", May 9 2013, page 31.

145 Gabe Moreen, Derek Walker and Kathleen Morris, Bank of America Merrill Lynch Equity Research, "Energy MLPs: Monthly sector presentation", May 9 2013, page 5.

146 Gabe Moreen, Derek Walker and Kathleen Morris, Bank of America Merrill Lynch Equity Research, "Energy MLPs: Monthly sector presentation", May 9 2013, page 4.

147 Gabe Moreen, Derek Walker and Kathleen Morris, Bank of America Merrill Lynch Equity Research, "Energy MLPs: Monthly sector presentation", May 9 2013, page 5.

148 Shira Ovide, The Wall Street Journal, Deal Journal, "Richard Kinder: The Luckiest Ex-Enron Employee", October 17 2011, Web, accessed January 13 2013, http://blogs.wsj.com/deals/2011/10/17/richard-kinder-the-luckiest-ex-enron-employee/

149 Kinder Morgan website, n.d., Web, accessed January 24 2014, http://www.kindermorgan.com/

150 Forbes Magazine, Special Edition, October 7, 2013, page 142.

151 Kinder Morgan, Press Release, "Kinder Morgan to Acquire KMP, KMR and EPB", August 10 2014, Web, accessed August 13 2014, http://www.kindermorgan.com/news/

152 Distrigas / GDF Suez website, n.d., Web, accessed March 4 2014, http://www.distrigas.com/ourcompanies/lngna-domac.shtml

153 Center for Climate and Energy Solutions, "Leveraging Natural Gas to Reduce Greenhouse Gas Emissions", June 2013, Web, accessed July 23 2013, http://www.c2es.org/publications/leveraging-natural-gas-reduce-greenhouse-gas-emissions

154 Ibid.

155 Jay Fitzgerald, The Boston Globe, "2 Costly LNG Terminals sit idle, January 23 2013, Web, accessed December 21 2013, http://www.bostonglobe.com/business/2013/01/23/offshore-gas-terminals-mass-bust-far/Qu8dyZzF6yBNAsDNaTT1ZJ/story.html

156 BP Statistical Review of World Energy, June 2013, Web, accessed July 31 2013, http://www.bp.com/content/dam/bp/pdf/statistical-review/statistical_review_of_world_energy_2013.pdf

157 Ibid.

158 Bloomberg News, "Reshaping Panama Canal Trade Means boom in U.S. Gas Flow to Asia", n.d., Web, accessed November 23 2013, http://www.bloomberg.com/news/2013-02-01/reshaping- panama-canal-trade-means-boom-in-u-s-gas-flow-to-asia.html

[159]   Reuters, U.S. Edition, "RPT-U.S. gas via Panama Frightens LNG Exporters Worldwide", September 5 2013, Web, accessed December 22 2013, http://www.reuters.com/article/2013/09/05/energy-lng-world-idUSL6N0H14D520130905

[160]   Transportation Energy Data Book, Oak Ridge National Laboratory, July 2013, accessed November 1 2013, http://cta.ornl.gov/data/tedb32/Edition32_Full_Doc.pdf

[161]   Ibid.

[162]   Center for Climate and Energy Solutions, "Leveraging Natural Gas to Reduce Greenhouse Gas Emissions", June 2013, Web, accessed July 23 2013, http://www.c2es.org/publications/leveraging-natural-gas-reduce-greenhouse-gas-emissions

[163]   Theenergycollective.com website, A New Debate Emerges: LNG or CNG for the Long Haul, July 16 2013, Web, accessed September 15 2013, http://theenergycollective.com/simonsylvesterchaudhuri/250096/new-debate-emerges-lng-or-cng-long-haul

[164]   Transportation Energy Data Book, Oak Ridge National Laboratory, July 2013, accessed November 1 2013, http://cta.ornl.gov/data/index.shtml

[165]   Ben Wojdyla, Popular Mechanics, "Should You Convert Your Car to Natural Gas?", February 10 2012, Web, accessed November 7 2013, http://www.popularmechanics.com/cars/how-to/maintenance/should-you-convert-your-car-to-natural-gas

[166]   Center for Climate and Energy Solutions, "Leveraging Natural Gas to Reduce Greenhouse Gas Emissions", June 2013, Web, accessed July 23 2013, http://www.c2es.org/publications/leveraging-natural-gas-reduce-greenhouse-gas-emissions

[167]   BP Statistical Review of World Energy, June 2013, Web, accessed July 31 2013, http://www.bp.com/content/dam/bp/pdf/statistical-review/statistical_review_of_world_energy_2013.pdf

[168]   Scott Sayles, Executive Consultant, Insights on Energy, Youtube.com video, "Shale or Tight Oil Processing", November 20 2012, accessed July 14 2013, http://www.youtube.com/watch?v=YbKaNsgAOyE

[169]   John Hageman, Twin Cities –Pioneer Press, "Soaring North Dakota crude production pushing crude to rails", February 1 2014, Web, accessed March 13 2014, http://www.twincities.com/business/ci_25042540/soaring-north-dakota-oil-production-pushing-crude-rails

[170]   Information Administration, Independent Statistics & Analysis, "Frequently Asked Questions", n.d., Web, accessed December 29 2013, http://www.eia.gov/tools/faqs/faq.cfm?id=29&t=6

[171] BP Statistical Review of World Energy, June 2013, Web, accessed July 31 2013, http://www.bp.com/content/dam/bp/pdf/statistical-review/statistical_review_of_world_energy_2013.pdf

[172] Energy Information Administration, Independent Statistics & Analysis, "Natural Gas" n.d., accessed September 22 2013, http://www.eia.gov/pub/oil_gas/natural_gas/analysis_publications/ngpipeline/index.html

[173] Center for Climate and Energy Solutions, Leveraging Natural Gas to Reduce Greenhouse Gas Emissions, June 2013, Web, accessed July 23 2013, http://www.c2es.org/publications/leveraging-natural-gas-reduce-greenhouse-gas-emissions

[174] Ibid.

[175] TransCanada Corporation, About the Project, "A proposed oil pipeline from Alberta to Nebraska", Web, accessed November 21 2013, http://keystone-xl.com/about/the-project/

[176] Harvard Magazine, "The Keystone XL Pipeline", November – December 2013, Web, accessed March 23 2014, http://harvardmagazine.com/2013/11/the-keystone-xl-pipeline

[177] Yale University, Yale Project on Climate Change Communication, "Public Support for Climate and Energy Policies In April 2013", April 2013, Web, accessed December 13 2013, http://environment.yale.edu/climate-communication/files/Climate-Policy-Support-April-2013.pdf

[178] Ibid.

[179] BloombergBusinessweek, "TransCanada Wins as Obama Keystone Permit Seen", November 8 2012, Web, accessed June 7 2013, http://www.businessweek.com/news/2012-11-08/transcanada-wins-as-obama-keystone-permit-seen

[180] Center for Climate and Energy Solutions, Leveraging Natural Gas to Reduce Greenhouse Gas Emissions, June 2013, Web, accessed July 23 2013, http://www.c2es.org/publications/leveraging-natural-gas-reduce-greenhouse-gas-emissions

[181] DeSmogBlog.com, "Antero Resources' Proposed $500 M Fracking Water Pipeline a Costly Wager for Drinking Water Supply, September 25 2013, Web, accessed October 23 2013, http://www.desmogblog.com/2013/09/25/antero-resources-s-proposed-500m-fracking-water-pipeline-costly-wager-drinking-water-supply

[182] Denver Business Journal / EnergyInc., "Antero Resources bets big on pipeline for water", August 14 2013, Web, accessed September 7 2013, http://www.bizjournals.com/denver/blog/earth_to_power/2013/08/antero-resources-bets-big-on-pipeline.html

[183] Ibid.

[184] United States Environmental Protection Agency, Overview of Greenhouse Gasses", n.d., Web, accessed October 17 2013, http://epa.gov/climatechange/ghgemissions/gases/ch4.html

[185] Center for Climate and Energy Solutions, Leveraging Natural Gas to Reduce Greenhouse Gas Emissions, June 2013, Web, accessed July 23 2013, http://www.c2es.org/publications/leveraging-natural-gas-reduce-greenhouse-gas-emissions

[186] United States Environmental Protection Agency, 40 CFR Part 63, "Oil and Gas Sector: New Source Performance Standards and National Emissions Standards for Hazardous Air Pollutants Review", April 17 2012, Web, accessed June 30 2013, http://www.epa.gov/airquality/oilandgas/pdfs/20120417finalrule.pdf

[187] Ibid.

[188] Ibid.

[189] Robert Kunzig, National Geographic News, "Climate Milestone: Earth's CO2 Level Passes 400 ppm", May 9 2013, Web, accessed July 27 2013, http://news.nationalgeographic.com/news/energy/2013/05/130510-earth-co2-milestone-400-ppm/

[190] Ibid.

[191] National Aeronautics and Space Administration, "NASA scientists react to 400 ppm carbon milestone", n.d., Web, accessed November 22 2013, http://climate.nasa.gov/400ppmquotes/

[192] Gallup Politics, "Climate Change: America's Views in 2014", March 12 2014, Web, accessed May 15 2014, http://www.gallup.com/poll/167843/climate-change-not-top-worry.aspx

[193] DSIRE, Database of State Incentives for Renewables & Efficiency, North Carolina Solar Center, March 2013, Web, accessed July 27 2013, http://www.dsireusa.org/documents/summarymaps/RPS_map.pdf

[194] United Nations Framework Convention on Climate Change, "Status of Ratification of the Kyoto Protocol", n.d., Web, accessed December 19 2013, https://unfccc.int/kyoto_protocol/status_of_ratification/items/2613.php

[195] University of East Anglia, "Global carbon emissions set to reach record 36 billion tones in 2013", November 19 2013, Web, accessed December 23 2013, http://www.uea.ac.uk/mac/comm/media/press/2013/November/global-carbon-budget-2013

[196] Fiona Harvey, Guardian News and Media Limited, theguardian.com, November 26 2012, "The Kyoto protocol is not quite dead", Web, accessed December 20 2013, http://www.theguardian.com/environment/2012/nov/26/kyoto-protocol-not-dead

[197] United States Environmental Protection Agency, "Overview of Greenhouse Gases", n.d., Web, accessed January 11 2014, http://www.eia.gov/environment/emissions/carbon/

[198] Ibid.

[199] Ibid.

[200] Intergovernmental Panel on Climate Change, "Climate Change 2013 The Physical Science Basis" September 2013, Web, accessed November 23 2013, http://www.climatechange2013.org

[201] Ibid.

[202] Ibid.

[203] Ibid.

[204] Ibid.

[205] USA Today, "Climate Change is Here and Now: Our View", October 14 2013, Web, accessed December 2 2013, http://www.usatoday.com/story/opinion/2013/10/14/climate-change-global-warming-ipcc-editorials-debates/2983979/

[206] John M. Brodder and Clifford Krauss, The New York Times, " New and Frozen Frontier Awaits Offshore Oil Drilling, May 23 2012, Web, accessed July 28 2014, http://www.nytimes.com/2012/05/24/science/earth/shell-arctic-ocean-drilling-stands-to-open-new-oil-frontier.html?pagewanted=1&_r=3

[207] The Wall Street Journal, Journal Reports: Energy, "Should the U.S. Finance Alternative Energy Startups", September 22 2013, Web, accessed December 24 2013, http://online.wsj.com/article/SB10001424127887324665604579078933691163714.html

[208] Ibid.

[209] Tesla Motors, Inc., Press Release, "Tesla Repays Department of Energy Loan Nine Years Early", May 22 2013, Web, accessed June 17 2013, http://www.teslamotors.com/about/press/releases/tesla-repays-department-energy-loan-nine-years-early

[210] Ibid.

[211] KPMG, Tax NewsFlash, No. 2013-07, "Energy-related provisions in American Taxpayer Relief Act of 2012", January 3 2013, Web, accessed January 30 2014, https://www.kpmg.com/U.S./en/IssuesAndInsights/ArticlesPublications/taxnewsflash/Documents/1307-jan3-2013-v2.pdf

[212] Timothy Cama, TheHill.com, "Manchin: Don't renew wind tax credit", June 16 2014, Web, accessed July 3 2014, http://thehill.com/policy/energy-environment/209572-manchin-dont-renew-wind-tax-credit

213   Energy.gov, "Business Energy Investment Tax Credit", n.d., Web, accessed December 29 2013,   http://energy.gov/savings/business-energy-investment-tax-credit-itc

214 Ibid.

215 Ibid.

216   Katie Fehrenbacher, GIGAOM.com, "Report: The clean power cash grant program was working", April 9 2012, Web, accessed July 17 2013, http://gigaom.com/2012/04/09/report-the-clean-power-cash-grant-program-was-working/

217 Energy.gov, "NREL Report Highlights Positive Economic Impact and Job Creation from 1603 Renewable Energy Grant Program", April 6 2012, Web, accessed June 12 2013,   http://energy.gov/articles/nrel-report-highlights-positive-economic-impact-and-job-creation-1603-renewable-energy

218 EnergyTransition.de website, Energy Transition, The German Energiewende, "Renewable Energy Act with feed-in tariffs", n.d., Web, accessed December 29 2013,   http://www.energytransition.de/2012/10/renewable-energy-act-with-feed-in-tariffs/

219 Energy Information Administration, Independent Statistics & Analysis, Today in Energy, "Feed in tariff: A policy tool encouraging deployment of renewable electricity technologies", May 30 2013, Web, accessed September 25 2013, http://www.eia.gov/todayinenergy/detail.cfm?id=11471

220   Eric Wesoff, Greentech Media, Germany Hits 59% Renewable Peak, Grid Does Not Explode" October 30 2013, Web, accessed December 13 2013, http://www.greentechmedia.com/articles/read/Germany-Hits-59-Renewable-Peak-Grid-Does-Not-Explode

221 Spiegel International Staff, SpiegelOnline International, "Germany's Energy Poverty: How Electricity Became a Luxury Good", September 4 2013, Web, accessed October 5 2013, http://www.spiegel.de/international/germany/high-costs-and-errors-of-german-transition-to-renewable-energy-a-920288.html

222 Ibid.

223 Ibid.

224 Ibid.

225   U.S. Department of the Interior, Bureau of Reclamation, Lower Colorado Region, Hoover Dam, "Frequently Asked Questions and Answers, n.d., Web, accessed January 25 2014, http://www.usbr.gov/lc/hooverdam/faqs/damfaqs.html

[226] Ibid.

[227] U.S. Department of Interior, Bureau of Reclamation, Lower Colorado Region, "Hoover Dam Frequently Asked Questions", n.d., accessed December 1 2013, http://www.usbr.gov/lc/hooverdam/faqs/damfaqs.html

[228] Terra-Gen Power LLC, Press Release, "Terra-Gen Power Announces Closing of $650 Million Construction Financing for Alta Wind VII & IX to Continue Build-Out of Nation's Largest Wind Energy Facility", April 17 2012, Web, accessed August 23 2013, http://www.terra-genpower.com/News/Terra-Gen-Power-Announces-Closing-of-$650-Million-.aspx

[229] Energy Information Administration, Independent Statistics & Analysis, Energy in Brief, "How much U.S. electricity is generated from renewable energy?", April 14 2014, Web, accessed April 15 2014, http://www.eia.gov/energy_in_brief/article/renewable_electricity.cfm

[230] Ibid.

[231] Federal Energy Regulation Commission, "Present Development of Conventional Hydroelectric Projects", June 10 2013, Web, accessed July 5 2013, http://www.ferc.gov/industries/hydropower/gen-info/regulation/present-dev.asp

[232] U.S. Department of Interior, Bureau of Reclamation, Lower Colorado Region, "The History of Hydropower Development in The United States", August 12 2009, Web, accessed October 15 2013, http://www.usbr.gov/power/edu/history.html

[233] Natural Resources Council of Maine, "A Brief History of Edwards Dam", n.d., Web, accessed January 23 2014, http://www.nrcm.org/projects-hot-issues/healthy-waters/edwards-dam-and-kennebec-restoration/a-brief-history-of-edwards-dam/

[234] Ibid.

[235] Water Power and Dam Construction Magazine, FERC orders removal of Edward's Dam in the U.S., January 28 1998, Web, accessed October 23 2013, http://www.waterpowermagazine.com/news/newsferc-orders-removal-of-edwards-dam-in-us

[236] Felicity Barringer, The New York Times, Environment, "Proposed Dam Presents Twin Conundrums in Alaska", March 6 2013, Web, accessed January 1 2014, http://www.nytimes.com/2013/03/07/science/earth/proposed-dam-presents-twin-conundrums-in-alaska.html

[237] Susitna Watana Hydro, "Diversifying Alaska's Energy Portfolio", n.d., Web, accessed January 23 2014, http://www.susitna-watanahydro.org/

[238]   ExxonMobil, BP, ConocoPhillips and TransCanada Press Release, "ExxonMobil, BP, ConocoPhillips and Alaska Pipeline Project Working Together to Commercialize North Slope Natural Gas", March 30 2012, Web, accessed December 23 2013, http://thealaskapipelineproject.com/docs/news_releases/20120330.pdf

[239]   State of Alaska, Gas Pipeline Project Office, n.d., Web, accessed February 23 2014, http://gasline.alaska.gov/sclng.html

[240]   Boualem Hadjerioua, Yaxing Wei and Shih-Chieh Koa, U.S. Department of Energy, Energy Efficiency & Renewable Energy, Wind & Water Power Program, "An Assessment of Energy Potential at Non-Powered Dams in the United States", April 2012, Web, accessed November 12 2013, http://www1.eere.energy.gov/water/pdfs/npd_report.pdf

[241]   National Hydropower Association, Developing Hydro, "Converting Non-Powered Dams", n.d., Web, accessed January 2 2014, http://www.hydro.org/tech-and-policy/developing-hydro/powering-existing-dams/

[242]   Boualem Hadjerioua, Yaxing Wei and Shih-Chieh Koa, U.S. Department of Energy, Energy Efficiency & Renewable Energy, Wind & Water Power Program, "An Assessment of Energy Potential at Non-Powered Dams in the United States", April 2012, Web, accessed November 12 2013, http://www1.eere.energy.gov/water/pdfs/npd_report.pdf

[243]   Ibid.

[244]   Emma Clark, Daily Mail, Mailonline, "Breathtaking Force: World's most powerful dam opens in China as gushing water generates the same power as Fifteen nuclear reactors", July 25 2012, Web, accessed July 23 2013, www.dailymail.co.uk/news/article-2178951/Three-Gorges-Worlds-powerful-dam-opens-China-gushing-water-generates-power-15-nuclear-reactors.html

[245]   American Wind Energy Association, Wind Industry Annual Market Report, U.S. Capacity and Generation, Year Ending 2013, Web, accessed April 30 2014, http://www.awea.org/AnnualMarketReport.aspx?ItemNumber=6305&RDtoken=35392&userID=

[246]   International Energy Agency, Technology Roadmap, Wind Energy, 2013 Edition, October 2013, Web, accessed March 15 2014, http://www.iea.org/publications/freepublications/publication/Wind_2013_Roadmap.pdf

[247]   American Wind Energy Association, Wind Industry Annual Market Report, U.S. Capacity and Generation, Year Ending 2013, Web, accessed April 30 2014, http://www.awea.org/AnnualMarketReport.aspx?ItemNumber=6305&RDtoken=35392&userID=

[248] Ibid.

[249] Ibid.

[250] Ibid.

[251] American Wind Energy Association, Wind Industry Annual Market Report, Manufacturing Facilities, Year Ending 2013, Web, accessed April 30 2014, http://www.awea.org/AnnualMarketReport.aspx?ItemNumber=6314&RDtoken=58041&userID=

[252] American Wind Energy Association, Wind Industry Annual Market Report, Turbine Manufacturers, Year Ending 2013, Web, accessed April 30 2014, http://www.awea.org/AnnualMarketReport.aspx?ItemNumber=6313&RDtoken=2958&userID=

[253] U.S. Energy Information Administration, Independent Statistics & Analysis, "Electric Power Monthly", March 2014, Web, accessed March 31 2014, http://www.eia.gov/electricity/monthly/pdf/epm.pdf

[254] American Wind Energy Association, Wind Industry Annual Market Report, State Capacity and Generation, Year Ending 2013, Web, accessed April 30 2014, http://www.awea.org/AnnualMarketReport.aspx?ItemNumber=6308&RDtoken=61755&userID=

[255] American Wind Energy Association, U.S. Wind Industry, Fourth Quarter 2013 Market Report, January 30 2013, Web, accessed March 5 2014, http://awea.files.cms-plus.com/FileDownloads/pdfs/AWEA%204Q2013%20Wind%20Energy%20Industry%20Market%20Report_Public%20Version.pdf

[256] Stephen Shankland, CNet.com, "Google X acquires kite power startup Makani", May 23 2013, Web, accessed June 26 2013, http://www.cnet.com/news/google-x-acquires-kite-power-startup-makani/

[257] Makani Power, Inc. website, n.d., Web, accessed January 23 2014, http://www.google.com/makani/

[258] Edison Electric Institute, Issues and Policies" Transmission", n.d., Web, accessed January 30 2014, http://www.eei.org/issuesandpolicy/transmission/Pages/default.aspx

[259] Google Investor Relations, "Google to Acquire Nest", January 13 2014, Web, accessed January 25 2014, https://investor.google.com/releases/2014/0113.html

[260] The Economist, Energy Storage, "Packing some power", March 3 2012, Web, accessed October 21 2013, http://www.economist.com/node/21548495?frsc=dg%7Ca

[261] U.S. Energy Information Administration, Independent Statistics & Analysis, "International Energy Outlook 2013, Web, accessed January 31 2014, http://www.eia.gov/forecasts/ieo/electricity.cfm

[262] Mark Luschini and Michael Halloran, Janney Montgomery Scott, "Global Infrastructure Outlook 2013", 2013, Web, accessed January 31 2014, http://www.janney.com/File%20Library/Unassigned/Outlook-2013_Infrastructure_4_2013.pdf

[263] Eric Wesoff and Herman Trabish, Greentech Media, "Lightsail Gets $5.5 M From Total, Thiel, Khosla, Gates for Compressed Air Energy Storage", February 19 2013, Web, accessed January 4 2014, http://www.greentechmedia.com/articles/read/LightSail-Gets-5.5M-from-Total-Thiel-Khosla-Gates-for-Compressed-Air-En

[264] Ibid.

[265] Lightsail Corporate Web Site, n.d., Web, accessed January 23 2014, www.lightsail.com

[266] Navigant Research, Press Release, "Compressed Air Energy Storage to Experience Dramatic Growth over the Next 10 years", August 19 2013, Web, accessed October 27 2014, http://www.navigantresearch.com/newsroom/compressed-air-energy-storage-to-experience-dramatic-growth-over-the-next-10-years

[267] Erin Ailworth, The Boston Globe, "Cape Wind project opponents file new lawsuit", January 22 2014, Web, accessed February 23 2014, http://www.bostonglobe.com/business/2014/01/22/opponents-file-new-suit-block-cape-wind-project/1T2Mh3zCza9LExTWzIYlXK/story.html

[268] Cape Wind Web Site, "Cape Wind Project Overview", n.d., Web, accessed May 2 2014, http://www.capewind.org/what/overview

[269] Ibid.

[270] Nick Juliano, E&E Reporter, Governors Wind Energy Coalition, "Mass. Regulators approve Cape Wind Power Contract", November 28 2012, Web, accessed January 2 2014, http://www.governorswindenergycoalition.org/?p=4027

[271] Ibid.

[272] Ibid.

[273] Ibid.

[274] Leigh Gilligan, Esq, Climate Lawyers Blog, McCarter & English, "The New Massachusetts Green Communities Act", October 2 2008, Web, accessed December

12 2013, http://www.climatelawyers.com/post/2008/10/02/_13_5_Million_for_the_ Massachusetts_Green_Communities_Act.aspx

[275] Ibid.

[276] Ibid.

[277] Molly Line, Fox News Politics, "Cape Cod community considers taking down wind turbines after illness, noise", February 26 2013, Web, accessed August 23 2013, http://www.foxnews.com/politics/2013/02/26/cape-cod-community-considers-taking-down-wind-turbines-after-illness-noise/

[278] Susan Donaldson James, ABC News, "'Wind Turbine Syndrome' Blamed for Mysterious Symptoms in Cape Cod Town", October 21 2013, Web, accessed December 24 2013, http://abcnews.go.com/Health/wind-turbine-syndrome-blamed-mysterious-symptoms-cape-cod/story?id=20591168

[279] Ibid.

[280] Ibid.

[281] Andy Webster, The New York Times, Movie Review, "Turbines in the Backyard: The Sound and the Strobes", February 2 2012, Web, accessed November 12 2013, http://www.nytimes.com/2012/02/03/movies/windfall-a-documentary-on-wind-turbines-by-laura-israel.html

[282] Town of Meredith, New York, n.d., Web, accessed January 25 2014, http://townofmeredith.com/about-meredith/

[283] Ibid.

[284] Ibid.

[285] Roger Ebert, Rogerebert.com, "Windfall", February 1 2012, Web, accessed August 23 2013, http://www.rogerebert.com/reviews/windfall-2012

[286] John Anderson, American Wind Energy Association, Into The Wind Blog, "Fact Check: Fox News Article To Put Wind Development in Context", January 2 2013, Web, accessed August 5 2013, http://aweablog.org/blog/post/fact-check-fox-news-article-fails-to-put-wind-development-in-context

[287] Ibid

[288] American Wind Energy Association, Wind Industry Annual Market Report, Manufacturing Facilities, Year Ending 2013, Web, accessed April 30 2014, http://www.awea.org/AnnualMarketReport.aspx?ItemNumber=6314&RDtoken=58041&userID=

[289] Merriam Webster, "insolation", n.d., Web, accessed December 23 2013, http://www.merriam-webster.com/dictionary/insolation

[290] National Renewable Energy Laboratory, "Photovoltaic Solar Resource of the United States", n.d., Web, accessed December 21 2013, http://www.entecsolar.com/Images/SolarIrradiation-UnitedStates.jpg

[291] Ibid.

[292] Ibid.

[293] Solar Energy Industries Association, "2013 Top Ten Solar States", n.d., Web, accessed April 14 2014, http://www.seia.org/research-resources/2013-top-10-solar-states

[294] Solar Energy Industries Association, Solar Industry Data, "U.S. PV Market Installs 4,751 Megawatts in 2013: Largest Year on Record", n.d., Web, accessed February 23 2014, http://www.seia.org/research-resources/solar-industry-data

[295] Ibid.

[296] Ibid.

[297] U.S. Energy Information Administration, Independent Statistics & Analysis, Electric Power Monthly, March 2014, Web, accessed April 1 2013, http://www.eia.gov/electricity/monthly/pdf/epm.pdf

[298] NobelPrize.org, The Nobel Prize in Physics 1921, n.d., Web, accessed October 23 2013, http://www.nobelprize.org/nobel_prizes/physics/laureates/1921/

[299] Las Vegas Sun "Some 200 Laid Off at North Las Vegas Amonix Solar Plant", January 25 2012, Web, accessed May 12 2014, http://www.lasvegassun.com/news/2012/jan/25/some-200-laid-north-las-vegas-amonix-solar-plant/

[300] IBISWorld, "Solar Panel Manufacturing in China: Market Research Report" April 2013, Web, accessed December 15 2013, http://www.ibisworld.com/industry/china/solar-panel-manufacturing.html

[301] Ibid.

[302] Wayne Ma, The Wall Street Journal, "China's Suntech to Stop Making Solar Panels", November 6 2013, Web, accessed January 2 2014, http://online.wsj.com/news/articles/SB10001424052702304448204579181100595519812

[303] Solar Energy Industries Association, Solar Industry Data, "U.S. PV Market Installs 4,751 Megawatts in 2013: Largest Year on Record", n.d., Web, accessed February 23 2014, http://www.seia.org/research-resources/solar-industry-data

304 Ibid.

305 Ibid.

306 Ibid.

307 Katie Fehrenbacher, Gigaom, Inc., "North Carolina has morphed into a solar power leader this year", December 20 2013, Web, accessed December 30 2013, http://gigaom.com/2013/12/20/north-carolina-has-morphed-into-a-solar-power-leader-this-year/

308 Todd Woody, The New York Times, "Solar Industry Anxious Over Defective Panels", May 28 2013, Web, accessed July 23 2013, http://www.nytimes.com/2013/05/29/business/energy-environment/solar-powers-dark-side.html?_r=0

309 U.S. Department of Energy, DSIRESOLAR, "Database of State Incentives for Renewables & Efficiency", n.d., Web, accessed January 18 2014, http://www.dsireusa.org/solar/solarpolicyguide/?id=17

310 PricewaterhouseCoopers, National Venture Capital Association, MoneyTree Report, Q2 2013, Web, accessed February 12 2014, http://www.pwc.com/en_U.S./us/technology/assets/moneytree-q2-2013-summary-report.pdf

311 Mercom Capital Group, "VC Funding in Solar Sector Down 50% in 2012", n.d., Web, accessed February 12 2014, http://mercomcapital.com/vc-funding-in-solar-sector-down-50-percent-in-2012-reports-mercom-capital-group

312 Dexter Johnson, IEEE Spectrum, "Nanowire Could Enable Solar Cells to Surpass the Shockley-Queisser Limit" March 26 2013, Web, accessed November 23 2013, http://spectrum.ieee.org/nanoclast/green-tech/solar/nanowires-could-enable-solar-cells-to-surpass-the-shockleyqueisser-limit

313 William Pentland, Forbes, "MLP Parity Act: Disrupting Distributed Energy" June 10 2013, Web, accessed January 24 2014, http://www.forbes.com/sites/williampentland/2013/06/10/mlp-parity-act-disrupting-distributed-energy/

314 Ibid.

315 ML Strategies LLC, "Master Limited Partnerships Parity Act", April 29 2013, Web, accessed August 17 2013, http://www.mlstrategies.com/articles/energy-4-29-13_MLP-Parity-Act-Summary--113th-Congress.pdf

316 PricewaterhouseCoopers, National Venture Capital Association, MoneyTree Report, Q2 2013, Web, accessed February 12 2014 http://mercomcapital.com/vc-funding-in-solar-sector-down-50-percent-in-2012-reports-mercom-capital-group

[317]   U.S. Energy Information Administration, Independent Statistics & Analysis, "China Country Analysis Brief Overview", May 30 2013, Web, accessed June 30 2013, http://www.eia.gov/COUNTRIES/country-data.cfm?fips=CH

[318]   Ibid.

[319]   http://www.eia.gov/analysis/studies/worldshalegas/

[320]   BP Statistical Review of World Energy, June 2013, Web, accessed July 31 2013, http://www.bp.com/content/dam/bp/pdf/statistical-review/statistical_review_of_world_energy_2013.pdf

[321]   Ibid.

[322]   Matthew Carr, Bloomberg, "China to Build More Renewables than EU, U.S. Combined, IEA Says", November 12 2013, Web, accessed December 15 2013, http://www.bloomberg.com/news/2013-11-12/iea-says-china-will-build-more-renewables-than-eu-u-s-combined.html

[323]   The World Bank, Data, "Energy Use (kg of oil equivalent per capita", n.d., Web, accessed January 20 2014, http://data.worldbank.org/indicator/EG.USE.PCAP.KG.OE

[324]   Keith Bradsher, The New York Times, "U.S. Solar Makers Say China Violated Trade Rules", October 19 2011, Web, accessed January 14 2013, http://www.nytimes.com/2011/10/20/business/global/us-solar-manufacturers-to-ask-for-duties-on-imports.html?ref=global&_r=0

[325]   Ibid.

[326]   Keith Bradsher, The New York Times, "U.S. and Europe Prepare to Settle Chinese Solar Panel Cases", May 20 2013, Web, accessed December 23 2013, http://www.nytimes.com/2013/05/21/business/global/us-and-european-union-set-to-negotiate-settlements-in-chinese-solar-panel-cases.html?_r=0

[327]   Keith Bradsher, The New York Times, "Six Companies Stay Anonymous in Solar Case", October 19 2011, Web, accessed November 27 2013, http://www.nytimes.com/2011/10/20/business/global/six-complainants-in-solar-trade-case-are-unnamed.html?ref=global

[328]   The New York Times, "Shift by U.S. muddles Solar Imports Case", May 17 2012, Web, accessed June 12 2013, http://www.nytimes.com/2012/05/17/business/global/shift-by-us-muddles-solar-imports-case.html

[329]   Ibid.

[330] Financial Times, "Chinese acquisitions in U.S. near record", n.d., Web, accessed December 23 2013, http://www.ft.com/intl/cms/s/0/893c76b4-ec44-11e1-a91c-00144feab49a.html#axzz2l2vulYTD

[331] Angel Gonzalez and Ryan Dezember, The Wall Street Journal, "Sinopec Enters U.S.", January 4 2012, Web, accessed December 12 2013, http://online.wsj.com/news/articles/SB10001424052970203550304577138493192325500

[332] Yvonne Lee, The Wall Street Journal, "Asian Energy Companies Continue to Look West", February 26 2013, Web, accessed November 13 2013, http://online.wsj.com/news/articles/SB10001424127887323384604578327354043148628

[333] Bloomberg New Energy Finance, "China's Power Sector Heads Towards a Cleaner Future", August 27 2013, Web, accessed November 23 2013, http://about.bnef.com/press-releases/chinas-power-sector-heads-towards-a-cleaner-future/

[334] Ibid.

[335] Ailun Yang and Yiyun Cui, World Resources Institute, Global Coal Risk Assessment, November 2012, Web, accessed November 2 2013, http://www.wri.org/publication/global-coal-risk-assessment

[336] Phys.org, "CO2 emissions +2.2% in 2012, driven by China and coal", November 19 2013, Web, accessed December 23 2013, http://phys.org/news/2013-11-co2-emissions-driven-china-coal.html

[337] Ibid.

[338] Michelle FloraCruz, International Business Times, November 19 2013, Web, accessed December 27 2013, http://www.ibtimes.com/smoking-air-pollution-creating-deadly-hazards-china-1-million-lung-cancer-patients-2025-1477180

[339] Kristina Chew, Environmental News Network, "China's Solution for Combating Air Pollution? Convert Coal to Synthetic Natural Gas", November 13 2013, Web, accessed December 12 2013, http://www.enn.com/environmental_policy/article/46681

[340] Ibid.

[341] Ibid.

[342] Global Wind Energy Council, Global Installed Wind Capacity, Yearend 2012, Web, accessed November 23 2013, http://www.gwec.net/wp-content/uploads/2012/06/Global-installed-wind-power-capacity-MW-%C3%94%C3%87%C3%B4-Regional-Distribution.jpg

[343] American Wind Energy Association, Wind Industry Annual Market Report, U.S. Capacity and Generation, Year Ending 2013, Web, accessed April 30 2014, http://

www.awea.org/AnnualMarketReport.aspx?ItemNumber=6305&RDtoken=35392&userID=

[344] The Wall Street Journal, "China Raises Target For Solar Power Capacity", July 15 2013, Web, accessed September 21 2013, http://blogs.wsj.com/chinarealtime/2013/07/15/china-raises-2015-target-for-solar-power-capacity/

[345] Feifei Shen, Bloomberg, Renewable Energy World, "China Confirms Goal for 35 GW of Solar Capacity by 2015", July 15 2013, Web, accessed December 17 2013, http://www.renewableenergyworld.com/rea/news/article/2013/07/china-confirms-goal-for-35-gw-of-solar-capacity-by-2015

[346] Ibid.

[347] American Wind Energy Association, Wind Energy Facts at a Glance, "U.S. Wind Energy Capacity Statistics, n.d., Web, accessed November 30 2013, http://www.awea.org/Resources/Content.aspx?ItemNumber=5059

[348] Solar Energy Industries Association, Solar Industry Data, "U.S. PV Market Installs 4,751 Megawatts in 2013: Largest Year on Record", n.d., Web, accessed February 23 2014, http://www.seia.org/research-resources/solar-industry-data

[349] United States Department of Labor, Mine Safety and Health Administration, Table 1., January – December 2012, Web, accessed January 12 2014, http://www.msha.gov/STATS/PART50/WQ/2012/table1.pdf

[350] Navigant Energy, "Impact of the Production Tax Credit on the U.S. Wind Market" December 12 2011, Web, accessed January 12 2014, http://awea.files.cms-plus.com/FileDownloads/pdfs/AWEA-PTC-study-121211.pdf

[351] Ibid.

[352] Andy Colthorpe, PVTECH, "U.S. Solar capacity to total 50GW by end of 2016, says Deutsche Bank", Web, accessed January 15 2014, http://www.pv-tech.org/news/us_installed_capacity_to_total_50gw_by_the_end_of_2016_including_20gw_to_30

[353] Ibid.

Acknowledgements:

Writing this book has been a labor of love. I could not, however, have completed it without the dedication and support of my Wife, Nancy, and my Daughter, Catarina. They have shown great patience and have indulged my love of writing and my fascination with the energy industry.

My editor, Allison Krupp, has played a vital, indispensable role in the development of this book's style and organization. She has done a great job bringing increased clarity to my writing and making the material more approachable for readers who are not energy-sector experts. She is a very talented writer and editor. I expect that she will have a very distinguished career in the years ahead.

Finally, I would like to thank my many friends and former colleagues on Wall Street and in the energy sector for providing their input and guidance on many aspects of this book. I am very fortunate to have worked with such high-quality professionals over the course of my career. A great many have offered their encouragement and support for this project and for that I am very grateful.

Index

www.ingramcontent.com/pod-product-compliance
Lightning Source LLC
Chambersburg PA
CBHW070924210326
41520CB00021B/6787